MEMOIRS OF A NAZARETH HOUSE GIRL

Anne Fothergill

Transporter Bridge, Middlesbrough.

ISBN: 978-1-907257-61-2

Published in 2013 by
Quoin Publishing Ltd.,
17 North Street, Middlesbrough,
England
TS2 1JP

Introduction

I wrote this memoir initially for my younger sister Eileen who was adopted – she never knew our mother or about my upbringing in Nazareth House – and also for my husband, three children and grandchildren.

I have never spoken openly about my life in the orphanage. I was ashamed to be known as a 'Nazzie House Girl'. It was a stigma back then. Now, with the distance of time, it does not bother me any more. I have come to terms with my past.

I don't have perfect recall of every piece of dialogue that took place. Some of the events are distant. What I'm recording here is the truth of what remains in my memory. Everything here reflects the reality of my childhood.

To protect the privacy of individuals a number of names and incidents have been changed.

CHAPTER 1

Early Memories

My earliest memory of life before I was put into the orphanage dates from when I was two-and-a-half years old.

I am sitting on a bedroom floor. I have crawled under the bed to reach my mother's magazines where she hides them from me. I am tearing the pages. I like the sound it makes. My mother normally tries to rescue the magazines from my grubby little fingers, but this time she ignores me. She has other things on her mind.

My thirteen-year-old brother Denis and my four-year-old sister Elizabeth are with me. My mother is bustling around opening drawers and slamming them shut. She seems to be in a hurry. She speaks to my brother. I sense that things are not good.

Later, it transpires that my mother is telling Denis that she is just nipping out to the shops. Denis suspects that she is not telling the truth as she has been packing a suitcase and is now carrying it as she makes her way out of the room.

I start to whimper. "Look after Anne," she says to Denis. If I had known that this day would change our lives forever I would have screamed the place down. It will be six years before I see my mother again.

Ten days later I am stood with Denis, Elizabeth and my

father Raphy on the doorstep of Nazareth House, an orphanage run by the Poor Sisters of Nazareth.

"Go and ring the door bell Denis, that's a good lad," Raphy says.

Denis presses hard on the shiny round doorbell. There is a tense wait and a sense of foreboding overwhelms me. I start to cry.

"Shush," my father says. "The nuns won't like you making that noise."

My brother picks me up and holds me in his arms.

After a while there is an unlocking of a latch. The heavy wooden door opens and a nun appears. She is dressed all in black, except for a white cloth framing her face.

"What do you want?"

"I'm Mr. Traynor and I've brought the two children," my father replies.

Her facial expression changes from a frown to a smile.

"Oh, of course. We were expecting you."

Denis puts me down gently. I am scared. I want my mother.

"Follow me and wipe your feet," the nun says as she leads the way into the parlour.

It is dark inside and there's an overpowering smell of wax polish. There are chairs situated on either side of the shiny polished floor.

"You may sit down if you wish," she says.

My father, Denis and Elizabeth sit down. But I remain standing as this strange place is unfamiliar to me.

A large picture of a man hangs on the wall. He is sat on a throne and is resplendent in red and gold. There is a small cap on his head and he is wearing spectacles. The nun notices that it has caught my interest.

"That is our Holy Father Pope Pius, a wonderful saintly man."

My father agrees.

"Are the children baptized?" she asks.

"Yes, Sister."

"I understand that their mother is not a Catholic."

"No, Sister, but I am."

"And what are the children"s names?"

"This is Elizabeth," he says pointing to my sister, "and the younger girl's name is Anne."

"Elizabeth and Anne are very good names. Elizabeth was the name of Our Lady's cousin," she says to my sister. "And you little one are named after Saint Anne, the mother of Mary."

She has a kind face even though she has no hair.

"So you are coming to stay with us for a while," she says as she takes Elizabeth and me by the hand. "Come along, I will take you to the playroom."

There are other children in the playroom. They stare at us. I keep tight hold of my brother's hand. "It's going to be okay," he says.

"You may stay with your sisters," she says to Denis, "while I talk to your father."

The room is big – so unlike the rented tiny two-bedroom terrace that my parents share with other lodgers.

Denis picks me up and plonks me on the long bench in the playroom. Elizabeth joins us. We sit there looking around us, unsure what to do until a nun comes over and

Elizabeth, me and Denis, 1950.

tells Denis to take us out to the playground.

Denis pushes me and Liz on the roundabout. This is fun. I haven't been on one before. Other children join us. "What's your name?" they ask. "Are you coming to live here?"

It is time to go back inside. Father is in the playroom with the nun from the parlour. She takes Elizabeth and me by the hand.

She whispers to my father, "You can leave now."

Father kisses us. "Goodbye," he says. "Be good." Denis gives me and Elizabeth a peck on the cheek. He walks backwards down the long corridor, waving at us all the while. I'm confused. My eyes are welling with tears. Sure he is going to come back. We can play on the nice roundabout until then. But he doesn't return. It will be years before I see him and we will never live as a family again.

Elizabeth and I are taken to the upstairs nursery. She stays one year with me in the nursery then is transferred downstairs to the main children's area. Although we know that we are sisters, we eventually lose the close bond that siblings normally share. We become just two of the many children who for unfortunate reasons have been taken in there.

Father visits us a few times at first and then his visits stop altogether. It will be many years before we see him or Denis again. And I will remain in Nazareth House until I am fifteen-years-old.

CHAPTER 2

Mornings

MAIN CHILDREN'S AREA.

"Kathleen Nelson, get the wet beds up."

These were the words that for many years woke me up in the morning.

Sister Wulstan was small. She had a wrinkled face, pale blue eyes that were hidden behind grey spectacles, and thin lips that hardly ever smiled. She always seemed to be in a bad mood. The nun's habit that she wore was too big for her, and she was forever hauling it up over the large belt that she wore around her waist. The girls thought her irritability was down to her getting on in age.

The routine was always the same. At five o' clock if you were awake you would hear the jangling of keys, the unlocking of a latch and a creaky door opening. Sister Wulstan would come out of her cell and into the dormitory. The lights would be switched on and then came the loud awakening. "Kathleen Nelson…"

Kathleen always took her time to reply. We were never sure if she was in a deep sleep or just pretending. Sister Wulstan's persistent calling would awaken most of the girls and some of them would get annoyed and shout:

"Kathleen, for god's sake get the smelly wet beds up."

Kathleen was fifteen years of age and was put in charge of the 'wet beds' because she had the misfortune of being one herself. It was her job to get the bed wetter up and lead them to the bathroom for a cold bath. They would then have to strip the sheets from their beds and put them in the laundry basket. All this was supposed to be done before any of the other girls were woken up. But the shouts of "Have you wet the bed?" and "Stinker" soon woke everyone.

The bright lights, the noise and the shouting so early in the morning put my nerves on edge. It was such a tumultuous start to the day that to this day, over fifty years later, I must have the lights dimmed and peace and quiet when I awake.

It was pointless trying to get back to sleep as half-an-hour later Sister Wulstan would return, clapping her hands and shouting.

"Get up. Get up. Get up." (She always said it three times.)

"You will be late for Mass."

She would go from bed to bed yanking back the curtains. She wasn't more than five feet in height and couldn't reach the top of the curtain rail, so she would grab hold of the bottom of the curtain and trail that with her as she moved along. The rosary beads that she wore around her neck would be swaying back and forth.

The cell where Sister Wulstan slept was a cordoned off area in the corner of the dormitory. None of the girls were allowed access to her room and it was kept locked. But on the odd occasion that she left it open, out of curiosity, we always peeped inside. The cell was sparse and contained a single bed which was covered in a white counterpane. There was a bedside locker which held a prayer book and a framed picture of Saint Teresa of the Roses, and on the wall above the bed hung a small crucifix.

Our dormitory consisted of two rows of single beds that were lined up on either side, rather like a military barracks, and beside each bed was a locker. The senior girls between the ages of fourteen to sixteen had curtains around their beds to give them some privacy.

There was a connecting door which took you through to another dormitory where Sister Mary was in charge, and she too had a cell in the corner of the room. Further along the passage there were similar dormitories and each had a nun in charge. There were no empty beds as there were lots of children in this home.

Shirley occupied the bed on my right and at fourteen was two years older than me. She was pretty but vain, with long fair hair which was tied up in a pony tail during the day. Now that she was classed as one of the senior girls she expected to be treated differently from us juniors. When Sister Wulstan approached she would hide under the bedclothes hoping 'Old Woolly Bags' (our nickname for Sister Wulstan) would leave her to get up in her own time. Sister Wulstan was having none of it, senior girl or not. Invariably, she would be at her bedside tugging at the counterpane.

"Get up. Get up. Get up, Shirley Egan or you'll be scrubbing the scullery floor for a week, you brazen hussy!"

She called you that for the slightest wrongdoing, so at one time or another we had all been labelled "brazen hussies." I don't think many of the girls knew what it meant.

"Why do we have to get up at this ridiculous hour?" Shirley grumbled. She was always tetchy in the mornings.

"How dare you talk back!" Sister Wulstan said. "I will report you to Sister Mary."

"Go on then," Shirley mumbled under her breath.

"What did you say, Shirley Egan? What did you say?"

Sister Wulstan would not tolerate any cheek whatsoever.

"The very idea of it," she would say if you answered back. "Just you wait until Sister Mary hears about this."

The bed at the other side of Shirley belonged to Penny, her best friend who was also the same age. She was slim with a pale face which gave her a delicate appearance. She was the quiet one, always deep in thought. She had an aunt who lived down south and would send her a letter now and again, but like most of us she had little contact with relatives.

Jeannie slept in the bed on my left. She had entered the orphanage a few years after me. She had two siblings but they were in care somewhere in Newcastle. She often had nightmares and would shout out in the night and frighten the life out of me. She had a bushy head of hair that she could hardly get a comb through. It caused her a lot of problems.

"Get that mop brushed," the nuns would yell at her.

"I c-can't h-help it." she would reply.

She was nervous and had a stutter which was more pronounced when she was upset or angry. It took guts to stand up to the nuns and it would certainly get you into bother. But Jeannie did it anyway. If she was told that she

9

would be fined one week's pocket money for answering back she would reply, "I d-don't c-care." But she did care and would end up in tears when she got no pocket money. We felt sorry for her.

"Poor Jeannie," we would say.

The twins Rosie and Bridie slept in the beds opposite me. Their mother had died and their widowed father was unable to look after them. He was almost crippled because of a war wound and leaned heavily on a walking stick to get around, but he visited them as often as he could.

The twins did not look alike; in fact you would find it hard to believe that they were even sisters. Rosie was tall with sallow skin, long dark hair and big brown eyes. Bridie was small, quite plump with fair curly hair and blue eyes. They were very affectionate and caring towards each other.

At bedtime the twins would say goodnight to each other and then they would argue about who would have the last word. We would lie in bed in the dark, laughing at their antics. Then a senior girl would shout out:

"For god's sake will you two shut up?"

Then another voice would call out and suggest that they should say goodnight together.

"All right then, after three – one, two, three."

"Goodnight Rosie." "Goodnight Bridie."

"Love you," they would shout together.

Then peace would prevail.

My bed was directly in front of the window and I could look out and see Albert Park which was situated across the road. I would watch the 'outside kids' carrying fishing rods or skipping their way through the tree lined paths. How I envied their freedom.

Albert Park had a large playing area with slides, swings and roundabouts. It also had a boating lake where rowing boats could be hired for up to half-an-hour. In the summer, we would lie in bed and listen to the boatman calling "time's up" through a megaphone. Many a night I fell asleep to the music coming from the roller-skating rink. Russ Conway's piano tunes were always popular with the skaters.

My favourite area of the park, though, was the little hills, where we would play hide and seek. It was sheer joy just to run up and down and shout and play.

We were not allowed out to the park very often and certainly not without a senior girl in charge. I remember lying on the wide expanse of grass looking up at the blue sky, soaking up the sun and praying that our mother would come and take me and Elizabeth home so that we could enjoy lots of days like these. Alas, it was never going to happen.

I was quite good at getting up in the morning, or rather I was determined that I would be out of the way before Sister Wulstan reached my bed. When I heard her shouting I would put one foot on the cold bare wooden floor, feel round for my slipper, put it on and hop about until I found the other one, then I was off to the bathroom. It was better to get in there before the rush started or you would have to wait for a wash basin and the water would be cold by then.

After getting the girls out of bed, Sister Wulstan would supervise the bathroom activities. The younger girls were put into groups under the charge of one of the senior girls. It was her responsibility to make sure that those in her group were washed, dressed and ready in time for Mass, otherwise she would be held responsible and that meant loss of privileges for herself. As a result, there were lots of shouting, name-calling and threats of "I'll box your ears if you don't get a move on."

There were two bathrooms but not enough wash basins, so there would be the inevitable pushing, shoving and shouts of "I was here first." Then a fight would break out.

There were three baths in each bathroom, and in the mornings they could only be used by those who had wet the bed. There was no hiding place for them. It would be especially humiliating for the older girls who were asked, "Why are you still wetting the bed at your age? You're just bone idle."

The general feeling was that it was due to laziness, and this added to the guilt and shame that the girls must have felt.

The mornings were hectic. There was always some nun or senior girl bellowing at you. "Stop that gossiping." "No dawdling." "Wash your face." "Don't forget to wash behind your ears." "Hurry up and get out of that bath."

It was the same each morning. No time to relax. Mustn't be late for Mass.

The nuns were very strict about your hair. Maybe it was because every now and again there would be an outbreak of nits. Then you would have to face the dreaded Jeyes treatment. This tar-coloured liquid came in a large navy blue tin and the smell was revolting. It would also be used to clean the drains. First it would be diluted in cold water in the wash basin. Then you had to rinse your head in it. It would really sting if it got into your eyes. The treatment would leave your scalp red and tender for days afterwards.

There was also a steel contraption called a Derbac comb. This would be used on a regular basis to check for any nits. Its blunt teeth would be scraped along your scalp and hair. It was torture.

The girls were allowed to have long hair. But it had to be plaited or tied up in two bunches with ribbons. The older girls opted for a ponytail.

If you were caught with your hair hanging loose you would get the 'monks haircut'. It was the nuns' specialty.

One day, I was playing tigs and my hair had fallen over my shoulders. I didn't get a chance to tie it back before Sister Mary saw me.

She was furious.

"Wait here," she ordered.

I knew what was coming and it was useless to protest.

"You've had it now, you'll get scalped," the girls said.

"Well, if it's short you won't have to bother with tying it up," Sister Mary said as she hacked at my hair with something like garden secateurs.

Nuns don't make good hairdressers. I didn't need to look in the mirror. I knew by the reaction of the other girls.

My sister was very angry.

"You'd think she had put a basin around your head," she said.

It would have been better if she had. At least it may have been the same length, but instead it was all up and down.

I had to go to school with my new haircut. The 'outside kids' stared at me.

I couldn't even boast that it was a new fashion in hair style. It was so awful that it would never have caught on.

The general consensus among the Nazareth House girls was that the nuns were bald and that's why they were jealous of our hair.

We did wonder if this was true as we only ever saw the nuns' faces and hands, and they wore long shapeless black dresses which covered their arms and came down to their ankles.

CHAPTER 3

Religious Duties and Beliefs

Mass was held in the church every morning at seven o'clock. If we wished to receive Holy Communion we had to have abstained from eating food for at least three hours. Because we had fasted from six o'clock the previous evening this wasn't a problem. We were allowed to have sips of water though if we felt faint.

The Mass was spoken in Latin which I didn't understand, and my concentration wasn't good especially at that time of the morning. I would be thinking about the chores I had to do, plus school and homework.

On special occasions such as a saints feast day, we had what was known as a 'singing' Mass which I preferred, as those of us who were in the choir could go upstairs and look down on the congregation below. Sister Mary played the organ and couldn't always see what was going on, so we had the freedom to have a natter in between the singing.

The church was within the grounds of the orphanage. In the summer we would walk across the yard from the children's accommodation, but in the winter or if it was raining we used the indoor passages.

We had our own priest, a Father Bickerstaffe who ministered all the religious services. He had served in the navy and had been older than the other priests when he was ordained.

He had a cheerful disposition and liked to sing. If he came by when we were in choir practice, he would get us to join him in singing one of the popular tunes of the day.

One of his favourites was "The Tiny House Song" which was very popular in the 1950s. He would sing the first line then we would sing the second and then we would join him in singing the chorus.

It was a pleasant interval from the tedium of hymn singing.

The church was quite small. Along the walls were colourful stained glass windows which depicted stories from the Bible or the lives of the saints. On one side of the altar there was a statue of Mary and on the other Saint Joseph holding the infant Jesus. My favourite statue was Saint Anthony. It was his youth and good looks that were appealing. There were other statues but they were mostly of old men with grey beards and a stern look on their faces.

The altar was made of white marble and on the front it had religious figures etched into it. The golden door of the tabernacle was kept so well polished that light seemed to radiate from it. The altar rails was also made of white marble which was cold to the touch. I remember shivering on my knees in the winter as I waited for the priest to give me Holy Communion.

At one side of the altar there was an enclosed area where most of the community of nuns would sit. We would only see them when they knelt at the altar to receive Holy Communion.

Nazareth House was a religious establishment run by the Poor Sisters of Nazareth, so our lives were governed by their rules and regulations. And attendance at the church services was obligatory.

We children would get bored and restless and would often be told to "face the front," and "stop fidgeting."

In those days there were no special allowances made for young children. You had to kneel alongside the adults and endure the long services.

As we got older, we were expected to know better and we had to behave in church or else you got a clip round the ear hole.

The religious services were endless. Mass was said every day and the Angelus was recited at noon. The Benediction service was held on Wednesdays and Sundays.

We had confessions on a Saturday. The Stations of the Cross were held frequently, especially during Lent. And the Rosary was said at the drop of a hat.

If the nuns wanted a special request granted we would say the Novena, which required prayers to be said over nine days.

We were often on our knees praying.

Every day of the year seemed to hold some religious significance for the nuns, usually it was a saints feast day. And much preparation went on beforehand for important occasions such as Christmas or Easter. This would mean endless hours of choir practice.

Sundays and feast days were called Holy Days of Obligation.

If you missed Mass on those days we were told you were guilty of having committed a mortal sin. Therefore, your soul would be 'stained' and you would have to go to confession to have it 'cleansed' before you could receive Holy Communion.

Venial sin was a less serious offence. Telling lies was in this category (unless it was a whopper) and to 'cleanse' your soul you only had to make an act of contrition.

We were taught that if you died with mortal sin on your soul you burnt in Hell. But if you died in venial sin you went to a place called Purgatory; there you would stay until you had atoned for your sins.

(I presumed that God decided how long your sentence would be.)

Babies who had died before they were baptised would remain in Limbo (wherever that was) for eternity.

There was a direct route up to Heaven for the saints, babies and young children – the latter two if they had been baptised.

To be told all of this as a child, I couldn't make sense of it.

I had visions of all these different 'places' floating around in the universe. Heaven was above us, somewhere beyond the clouds.

Hell was below, and if that's where you ended up for just missing Mass on a Sunday then it must have been overcrowded down there.

I did not look forward to Good Friday. The service was long and tedious and all the statues and religious icons would be covered with a purple cloth, and we were not allowed to speak for long periods of the day. It was always a depressing time and it carried on through Easter Saturday.

But then, on Easter Sunday, there would be much rejoicing and the choir in the church sang "Hallelujah."

The quiet of the last couple of days would be replaced by the noise of the girls gabbing amongst themselves and laughing. Even the nuns seemed more relaxed.

Afterwards a special breakfast was laid on and for a change we could have cornflakes instead of porridge, and as a treat black pudding and a type of sausage called red 'paloney.'

At dinner, we were allowed to have 'minerals' such as orange juice or lemonade.

March 17th was the Feast Day of Saint Patrick and we sang the hymn "Hail Glorious Saint Patrick" at the Mass.

Because most of the nuns were Irish, there was much celebration. Shamrock would be brought over from Ireland and proudly wore while pinned to the nuns' habits. In the evening, the older girls who had left school would attend a Saint Patrick's dance at the local church hall.

There were no such celebrations on Saint George's Day.

November 1st was the feast day of All Saints. It was a Holy Day of Obligation. At the Mass we had to stand while the Litany of Saints was read out. The list seemed to get longer every year.

November 2nd was All Souls Day. There was a belief amongst the girls that the souls of the dead would visit you on that night. Apparently, they would tap you on the shoulder to awaken you.

"What do souls look like?" I asked one of the senior girls.

"They are invisible," she said.

I was totally confused. So I might be woken up by something that I couldn't see? That was scary.

We would be lying in bed in the dark, and one of the girls would be telling ghost stories. We were too frightened to go to sleep, and when we did eventually drop off we"d have nightmares. Quite a few of us wet the bed on those nights.

At Christmas we would attend Midnight Mass, and all the carols that we had rehearsed in choir practice would be sung. We always started with "Come, Come, Come to the Manger."

I joined the choir when I was eleven years of age. I didn't have a choice – if you could sing a musical note, you were in.

After school or at the weekend we would endure long hours of choir practice. There was always a new hymn to learn for a saints feast day (and there were many).

The choir practice sessions could go on for hours. If you sang a wrong note or were not paying attention, Sister Mary would tap you on the head with a bamboo cane. We practiced until she was satisfied that we knew every word and were singing in harmony.

We had our amusing moments though. One day a nun who was quite elderly asked Sister Mary if she could play the organ at the midweek Benediction service.

She didn't know how to pull out the correct stops on the organ and asked Rita, one of the senior girls, if she would do it for her. Rita deliberately pulled out the wrong ones.

At Benediction the nun was playing the organ. She was leaning forward and squinting as she tried to read from the music sheet. Her feet were on the pedal board and her hands were going up and down the keyboard. But there seemed to be no co-ordination and she kept striking the wrong notes. It created such a din but she carried on regardless.

There was much giggling among the girls but Sister Mary was furious.

CHAPTER 4

Chores

After the Mass we had breakfast which was usually porridge with sausage or bacon with fried bread and tea. We had three meals a day and a light supper. We all had to have a tablespoon of cod liver oil every week, followed by a tablespoon of Virol which was sickly sweet and looked like liquid toffee. But it took away the fishy taste of the cod liver oil.

When I was older and was classed as a senior girl I was responsible for keeping a record of all the meals that we consumed. I had to keep a food diary. This would be shown to the inspectors when they paid a visit to the home.

When breakfast was finished we all had our duties to attend to before we went to school. We had to work in groups of three or four depending on the task.

There were breakfast plates to wash, tables to be wiped down and re-laid, dormitories to be cleaned and beds to be made,

The floors also had to be waxed and polished. There was rather a comical way of polishing the floor. A thick type of cloth which we called a 'polisher' would be put under one foot. Then we would link arms across each others' backs rather like the Tiller Girls at the London Palladium and we would move up and down and around the tables.

With cloth underfoot we'd go from side to side and top

to bottom, making sure that we covered the whole floor. When we had finished polishing the dining room floor we would continue out along the passages. To keep in step we would sing. One of our favourite songs was "The Happy Wanderer" because it had a good rhythm to move along to.

Looking back now it was hilarious, although we didn't think so at the time – it was just the norm. One task that I detested was washing up. There were so many greasy plates and dishes to wash that by the time you had finished the water would be cold. There would be a large scum mark left round the rim and the sink had to be clean and tidy before you set off for school.

It was all go in the mornings, but in between doing the chores we would be finding out the latest gossip about other girls until we'd be told to "stop tittle tattling," and "get on with your work."

The chores had to be finished in time for school or your name could be written in Sister Mary's book.

You could also be ordered to scrub the scullery floor for a week as a punishment. This was a mucky job. The scullery was large and everyone would use it. So the floor was dirty, greasy and covered in spillages.

We would be on our knees on the cold floor, scrubbing away with a scrubbing brush that had been coated with green household soap. Then the floor had to be rinsed and wiped over with a cloth. By the time you had finished you had sore knees and crinkled fingers.

Mari Carr was in my group so we often did our chores together. She had been in the orphanage from when she was young and had come through from the nursery as I had. She was the same age as me and had short mousy hair, brown eyes and skin that looked permanently tanned. Mari was rebellious and this would often get her into trouble. She did the things that I would have liked to do but didn't have the nerve. I was no angel though. I didn't need much encouragement to get into mischief, though I knew when to toe the line. But Mari was confrontational and wouldn't back down. She always had to have the last word

"Look at my hands, the skin's peeling," Mari would grumble if it was her turn to wash the dishes.

"Swap places will you? I'll give you some of my pocket money."

She was always trying to bribe the girls who were doing the drying. Most of us just got on with the chores but Mari was always looking for a way out. "She's a bad influence," the nuns would say.

She always had a crush on some film star or rock and roll singer whom she was going to marry when she left Nazareth House. She would tuck her school blouse in to emphasise her breasts and she was always talking about boys. Mari didn't learn anything about the birds and the bees from the nuns at Nazareth House. She was getting snippets of information in the playground at school, especially from Marlene – one of the 'outside' girls who was worldly for her age and seemed to know it all. Mari would then brag about what she had learned and then she was accused of being common by some of the girls.

"She is man daft," they would say. But really she was like most of us, just curious.

There was no rest at the weekends. On Saturday we

would be ordered to help in the laundry, where it was so hot that beads of sweat would drip from your forehead. And when the steam roller was going full blast you could barely see each other in the mist.

The laundry was in a separate building but still within the grounds of Nazareth House. It housed all the machinery that was needed to wash the clothes, bed linen and towels for the residents of the home. There were large washing machines, spinners and dryers, and also a giant steam roller for ironing the damp sheets. Overhead there would be wooden pulleys laden with damp washing.

The very dirty laundry had to be pre-washed in cauldrons of boiling green slime. The colour came from the copious amounts of bars of green Fairy soap that was used. There was also a tub for starching the nuns' wimples. If they were not starched to the nuns' satisfaction they would be sent back to be redone.

If the weather was fine the washing would be put outside to dry but it was a laborious task. There was always loads of washing to be hung on the clotheslines and we used lots of wooden dolly pegs.

Lizzie was in charge of the laundry. She was in her forties and had been in Nazareth House since she was very young. She was muscular and strong and this enabled her to lift the heavy clothes baskets. She had a ruddy complexion and grey straggly hair and she didn't talk much except to give orders.

"Don't put your hands in the hot water, use the tongs," or "Take the clothes out of the spin dryer."

But it was so noisy anyway it was difficult to have a

conversation. The constant clanging of the clothes dryers and the whirring of the washing machines together with the screeching of the spin dryers would leave you with a bad headache.

CHAPTER 5

Nuns and Missionaries

The Community of Nuns shared responsibilities. Some looked after tiny babies and children, or the old folk. Others supervised the kitchen, laundry or had various other duties. Quite a few of the nuns went begging door to door for donations. There were many nuns so we did not get to know them all, only those in our immediate circle. There was a Mother Superior who had overall responsibility for everyone in Nazareth House.

Sister Mary was in charge of the children whose ages ranged from five upwards. She was the main supervisor and if anyone misbehaved they were sent to her. She had a pleasant face and she spoke with a soft Irish lilt. It was difficult to know her age but she wasn't as old as Sister Wulstan. She could be quite charming and was very popular with the Mother Superior and some of the other nuns. She had her favourites and if you were in her good books she was nice to you. The girls either liked or loathed her. I was fortunate in that I was one of her 'pets'. This is what the girls called you if she singled you out to run errands for her. I had neat handwriting so she chose me to write thank you letters to our benefactors. It could be quite nerve wracking though as she stood over me, making sure I made no spelling mistakes.

She was strict, but there was a fun side to her as well. I

remember her playing a game of rounders on the beach at Redcar, laughing as she ran to beat the ball, her veil billowing in the wind. I suppose like most of the other nuns she put up a front and we never really got to know her true character.

She was optimistic though and believed in miracles and the power of prayer.

"If you pray hard enough your request will be granted," she would say and would have us reciting endless decades of the Rosary.

One time she had us praying for a minibus so that we children could have more days out.

I had visions of one being floated down to earth. Amazingly, a minibus was donated to Nazareth House but by then both I and Sister Mary had left the orphanage.

We received our pocket money from Sister Mary on Saturdays and we looked forward to going to our local shop, Spennies. We would buy gobstoppers, love hearts and kaylie sherbet which you sucked through a liquorice tube.

The amount of pocket money you received depended on your age. The senior girls got a little bit more than the younger girls.

Sister Mary would keep a record of all misdemeanours, and if your name was in her book you would pay a fine which would come out of your pocket money at the end of the week. The list of things that you could be fined for seemed endless: late for Mass; chores not finished; talking in church; being cheeky; even singing a wrong note in choir practice. Some weeks you would have nothing left to spend once the fines had been paid. If you were unlucky you would continue to owe money on the following week's pocket money. There was sub money deducted if we were in the Girl Guides and/or The Legion of Mary. We also had to pay for our own toothpaste. It was pink and came in a round tin with the name Gibbs on the lid.

Sister Agnes was what we in the North would call 'canny'. The youngest of the nuns, she had only recently been ordained. She was not very tall, so some of the older girls towered above her. Her "eyes were as blue as the sky" (we would tell her) and she had a round cheery face with rosy cheeks.

She had come from a farming background and spoke with a Southern Ireland accent. I could imagine her out in the fields, fussing over the lambs as she was soft and gentle. The older nuns were always bossing her around.

"Sister Agnes, would you supervise the children in the playground."

"Darn the socks."

"Get the children upstairs to bed."

"Check that all lights are out and lock up."

She was Cinderella all right but there was no prince coming to rescue her. Still, she accepted it all cheerfully.

"Yes Sister, I'll be doing that as soon as I have finished," she would say. Or, "Holy Mother of God, is that the time already Sister?"

Sister Agnes was popular and you could confide in her to some extent. When things were said to her that she found incredulous she would utter, "God bless us and save us."

Now and again we would have priests who came to

supervise the religious retreats. They were usually from a missionary order that was based overseas. These retreats were a welcome distraction from our everyday lives.

One priest who came to organise the retreat caused quite a stir. He was young, suntanned and he wore a long brown dress. He had sandals on his feet and no socks. Mari was in seventh heaven.

"Ooh, isn't he dishy." That seemed to be the 'in' word.

"You can't talk about a priest like that," said Bernadette Keats, who at fifteen was one of the senior girls and quite religious, (well she could recite the Catechism backwards). We expected her to become a nun herself one day.

"It's a sin, isn't it Sister Agnes, to have impure thoughts about men?" It was quite a common notion among some of the girls and the nuns that if you seemed overly interested in the opposite sex you were seen as a trollop. And therefore destined for a life of debauchery.

There was no sex education either in the home or at school.

When a girl started their periods she was given a book titled 'Mary the Virgin Mother.' There was no mention of sexual intercourse or how babies were conceived. That subject was taboo! What girl would have had the nerve to ask any of the nuns? You'd have to be a 'brazen hussy' to do that. Although some of the girls were at an age and biologically able to have babies, they were ignorant of how it came about.

"I only said that he was dishy," Mari said.

"That is an inappropriate way to talk about Father Francis," Sister Agnes said sternly.

"Ooh, is that his name? He is lovely though Sister, isn't he? If you weren't a nun would you marry him?"

Mari enjoyed teasing Sister Agnes. She wouldn't have dared say that to any other nun.

"Mari Carr you should go to confession and ask for forgiveness."

"What for, Sister?" Mari asked, feigning innocence.

"Aren't priests and nuns allowed to marry?"

"Certainly not, and you cannot talk about one of God's holy men in that way," Sister Agnes said, blushing profusely.

"God bless us and save us."

I enjoyed the religious retreats. They would last from one to three days and consisted of talks, prayer and meditation. The theme of the day would be on something like forgiveness. The missionary would talk about the Parable of the Prodigal Son. Then we were expected to go around expressing our forgiveness to everyone you thought you had 'sinned' against, and they in return were expected to forgive you.

I don't remember any of the girls going up to one another and saying, "I forgive you." Now that would have been seen as too holy. If you forgave any of the other girls it had to be between you and your maker.

Heaven forbid if any of the bullies like Cowan had found out that you had forgiven them. You'd have been seen as a soft touch and used as a punch bag.

No, it was better to hold a grudge and scheme of ways to get your own back. To hell with forgiveness.

I especially enjoyed the missionary telling us about Africa and his work among the poor. They would also talk about the life and times of their favourite saint, usually the one that their order was named after.

We were supposed to remain silent in between the prayers and meditation. But this meant that we had to be quiet for long periods of the day and that was difficult for some of us.

We were allowed out into the play area, weather permitting, but we had to go around in silence. It was great to have the freedom of not having to do anything but pray. There would be notes passed between the girls and lots of giggling. Although if you saw any of the nuns you would put your head down and pretend that you were lost in prayer and meditation.

CHAPTER 6

Ringworm

On Saturdays we would have our head examined by one of the nuns.

She would be seated on a chair with a towel over her knees. We had to kneel down in front of her while she gingerly examined our hair. If she told you that you were clean there would be audible sighs of relief.

But if she ordered you to "Stand over there," you knew then that you had unwelcome visitors.

If you were found to have nits another girl would have the unenviable task of removing them. The 'crawlers' would be squashed on her finger nail.

"Ooh that one was still alive, that's disgusting," she would say.

We were rather like monkeys grooming each other.

I was about eight-years-old and waiting in line to have my hair examined when an agitated Sister Mary came in to the washroom.

"There has been an outbreak of ringworm. I want anyone who is found to be infected to be kept apart from the other girls."

Recently, a family had been admitted to the home. They were found to have ringworm – a contagious fungus infection of the skin. We shared the same combs so it was inevitable that the infection would spread. And it did. I was infected, as were Dot and Helen Dugan (who were sisters) and Josie Mitchum.

I was excited when I was found to have ringworm, especially as we were told that we would not be able to go to school. But I would not have been so glad had I known then that the 'treatment' would leave me scarred for life.

We four were instantly isolated from the others and taken across the yard to the old folk's home.

The old folk's home was at the other end of Nazareth House, well away from the children's area. The residents were men and women who could no longer work or they were getting on in years. The men's living quarters were downstairs and the old ladies were on the upper floor. Some of the old women had spent all their lives in Nazareth House.

We were placed under the care of Sister Luke, who was in charge of the old ladies.

She took us to meet Miss Sleightholme, who was responsible for mending the clothes that needed repairing. The other ladies slept in dormitories but she had a room all to herself.

When we entered her room she was sitting at a sewing machine. She must have been expecting us as she was not alarmed to see four children being herded into her room. Peering down over her glasses, she looked at us.

"Good afternoon children," she said cheerfully.

There was only one chair in the room so we were told that we could sit on her bed.

Suddenly, Josie jumped up from the bed.

"What's that?" she shouted.

Something soft and furry had brushed past her leg. It was a striped cat and it had crept out from under the bed.

"That's Tabby," laughed Miss Sleightholme. "She's just being friendly, she sleeps under my bed.

"You will have to meet Sooty, he's a cheeky chappie."

Miss Sleightholme loved cats. She had four and they were all strays. There was Tabby, Sooty, Socks (because he had white paws) and Yorkie. The latter was named because Miss Sleightholme was proud of her Yorkshire roots.

She had never married and had worked as a tailoress during her working life. When she had retired she had chosen to live at Nazareth House. I wondered why anyone would want to come and live there voluntarily. I would never do that.

Her room was cramped and it was used for both sleeping and working. There was a single bed, a chest of drawers and a small bedside locker on which stood a small statue of Our Lady of Lourdes. The large Singer sewing machine was in the corner of the room. There were wicker baskets piled high with clothes, with 'to be repaired' labels attached to them. Rolls of material of various shades were stacked in one corner of the room. And a large bag overflowing with balls of wool and knitting needles lay on the end of the bed.

On the wall nearest to her bed was a picture of the crucifixion. The splattered red blood oozing out of the hands, feet and side of the crucified Christ made it particularly gruesome. It would have given me nightmares looking at that last thing at night.

Statuettes of the various saints were placed along the

window sill. And if you looked out of the window you could watch people go in and out of the popular Rea's Café.

Sister Luke looked at her pocket watch.

"I will have to go now or I'll be late for vespers."

She smiled at Miss Sleightholme.

"I will leave the girls with you and I'll call back after prayers."

"Be good," she said to us as she left the room, closing the door behind her.

Miss Sleightholme removed her spectacles. She squinted at us through teeny eyes.

"Do you know why you are here?" she asked with a bemused smile on her face. She wasn't used to having children around.

"We've got ringworm," Dot said. "It's on me head."

And she parted her hair to show where the offending fungus had formed a circular ring on her scalp.

"It's dead itchy Miss," she said.

Miss Sleightholme slightly recoiled.

"You don't have to show me dear, that won't be necessary," she said.

"Do you know why Sister has brought you to me?" she asked, looking from one girl to another.

"Are you going to show us where we will be sleeping?" Helen asked hopefully.

"No my dear, I am sure Sister Luke will do that when she gets back from vespers."

"We're only gonna be here for about a week, aren't we Miss?" Dot asked.

"I'm afraid you will be here for quite some time. Maybe a few months."

"A few months?" Dot gasped.

We were all startled. Miss Sleightholme continued.

"It's quite a serious infection and may require weeks of treatment."

I didn't understand 'treatment' – did that mean using ointment? My head started to itch. I was feeling nervous. And worse was to come.

She asked Dot to bring the chair over to her. Then she perched herself on the seat, clasped her podgy hands together and told us exactly why we had been brought to her room.

Apparently, we were all going to have our heads shaved that afternoon and Miss Sleightholme had been asked to make hats for each of us to cover our bald heads.

"I'm not going to have my head shaved!" Dot shouted hysterically while shaking her dark curly hair.

"Nor me," Helen retorted, who had the same lustrous curls as her sister.

I was trying to imagine myself with a bald head. Will my hair grow back? I wondered.

Josie must have been thinking the same thing because she nervously asked Miss Sleightholme:

"Will we be bald for ever?"

"No. No, of course not. It will grow back my dear.

"And it may even grow back curly," she said, looking at Josie's 'rats tails'.

The Dugan girls were not so sure; they didn't want 'other' curls. They were quite happy with the ones they already had.

Miss Sleightholme went over to a chest of drawers and took out a tape measure.

"Now then, who's first?" she asked.

We gawped at her. No one answered.

"It won't hurt," she said reassuringly. "I am only going to measure around your head."

I was the youngest so she chose me to go first. She put the tape measure around my head and asked me my name.

"Oh, did you know that Saint Anne was the mother of Our Lady?"

"Yes."

The nuns had told me many times.

It was an honour to be named after a saint, they'd said. I had a lot to live up to.

My father had given me the name Anne. But my mother told me later that if she'd registered my birth she would have called me Jeanette after Jeanette MacDonald. She and Nelson Eddy were a popular singing duo at the time. I would have much preferred to have been called Jeanette, as it sounded so much more glamorous than plain Anne.

Later that afternoon, I had my head shaved. It left me completely bald. But I didn't cry or make a fuss when I lost all my golden curls. Saint Anne would have been proud of me.

We four 'lepers' were soon ensconced into everyday life with the old ladies. We had our own bedroom and the sheets on our beds were changed every day. We ate our meals with the old folks in the dining room but we had to sit at our own table. Some of the old ladies were kind and gave us sweets. Others frowned – they were annoyed that four noisy girls were disturbing their once peaceful lives.

Miss Sleightholme made two hats for each girl, one for everyday use and one for Sunday. They were old-fashioned and rather like the hats worn in Jane Austen's era.

At first, living with the old folks was fun. Everything was different. We did not attend school and had no chores to do. Every morning and evening we had ointment applied to the infected areas on our scalp. This would be done by one of the nuns who would inform us if the sores were healing.

The rest of the day would be spent idling the hours away in the day room. In those early days, we were not allowed outside but we still had to attend Mass every Sunday. We were seated at the back of the church, well away from the other children. We must have looked like freaks in our silly hats because they stared at us as they walked up the aisle.

One day, Miss Sleightholme's cat Tabby had kittens. They were in a box under her bed. Josie and I were bored and we decided to go and see them. The door to her room was ajar but when I knocked there was no answer. We could hear the kittens mewing. Josie put her head round the door.

"Miss Sleightholme's not here," she said. "Let's have a peep at the kittens."

I hesitated. Should we go in her room when she wasn't in? I had never done it before.

"Go on, I dare you," Josie said.

I shouldn't have been such a show off.

I crept over to the bed, knelt down on one knee and lifted the counterpane.

In the dark I could just make out a couple of tiny kittens nestled together.

I was about to pick up the little black one that looked a lot like Sooty, when in a flash a bundle of stripes darted out from under the bed. It attacked me, scratching my hand. I screamed, got up and ran out of the room. Josie heard me, and started running down the passage. I followed her with the cat chasing me. Tabby caught up with me and scratched the back of my ankle. I yelped.

A couple of the old ladies came out of the dormitory to see what all the commotion was about. One used her walking stick to stop Tabby in her tracks and shooed her back to Miss Sleightholme's room.

I was shaking after the ordeal and Miss Sleightholme gave Josie and me a right telling off.

It was the main talking point at the evening meal, and I got lots of attention from the old ladies when I showed them my scratched hand and ankle. The reactions were mixed.

"Vicious creature," one lady said sympathetically.

"Cat's shouldn't be allowed in the home," another said.

Most sided with Miss Sleightholme.

"Well, you have only yourself to blame."

"Tabby was only defending her young."

Helen and Dot responded well to treatment and soon they were allowed to rejoin the other children in the main area. Josie and I were not doing so well, and one morning we were told that we'd be going to the Carter Bequest Hospital to have special treatment on our scalps.

At the hospital, purple crosses were dotted around my scalp to pinpoint the areas to be treated. I was shown into a room that was rather like an operation theatre.

I had to lie on the bed with a beam of light aimed at my head. The nurse would leave me on my own in the room. The heat and the gentle pinging from the machine helped me relax and I would often fall asleep. I had to have a few sessions spread over the weeks.

But the treatment ended when it was found that the dosage had been too high and it had actually burnt my scalp. I remember my head feeling sore and tender for weeks afterwards. And I was left with a bald patch which I still have to this day.

Eventually, the infection cleared up and I was allowed to go back to the children's accommodation.

CHAPTER 7

Mother

Elizabeth and I were fortunate that we had each other. Although I was closer to girls of my own age, she would still look out for me and tried to protect me when I was being bullied by a senior girl.

One day she even had to protect me from the Mother Superior. Something had happened and I cannot even remember the incident, but somebody had put the blame on me. I heard Mother Superior shouting out my name: "Anne Traynor. Where is she? Just wait until I get hold of her, the little madam."

I was wondering what I had done wrong. She had come flying down the passage like a bat out of hell. Believe me, for a young child there is nothing as frightening as the sight of a nun dressed all in black, red in the face, incandescent with rage with her rosary beads rattling ominously, whose sole aim is to find you and probably give you a good hiding. I was terrified and was shaking like a leaf. My sister grabbed me and pushed me into the room. She told me to hide behind the cupboard.

One of the girls, Bernadette Kirwin, saw me and my sister asked her not to give me away. Thankfully she didn't. Mother Superior stormed into the room, demanding to know where I was. What was most surprising is that she didn't know who I was and any one of the girls could have said they were me. I hid for a while, my heart racing, until Mother Superior went back to her own quarters. The episode was soon forgotten. I do not know to this day what all the fuss was about. But I still shudder when I think about it. Saint Anne must have been looking after me that day. Fortunately, not all the Mother Superiors were like her. She was one of the cruel ones.

I was eight years of age and Elizabeth was ten when our own mother came to visit for the first time since leaving us all those years ago. I remember the day so well. It was four o'clock in the afternoon and I had just got off the bus after returning from Saint Mary's Primary School. I was making my way through the back entrance of Nazareth House when I heard someone call my name. I must be in trouble I thought, but had no idea why so I kept my head down and hid behind the girls in front of me.

"Anne Traynor, where are you?" I didn't reply.

Someone grabbed my jumper from behind and wouldn't let me go. It was the bully Judy Cowan. She wasn't very popular and many of the girls were frightened of her. She often got into fights and was always threatening to give someone a good hiding.

"I've got her Kathleen, she's trying to hide," she said spitefully.

Kathleen Nelson came running over.

"Oh there you are," she panted. "I've been looking all over for you. Sister Mary wants to see you."

"What for?" Now I was scared.

"Your mother's here."

"My mother?" I was astounded.

Cowan let go of me.

"Come on, Sister Mary sent me to get you," Kathleen said as she took my hand.

I was in a daze. No-one had mentioned my mother in all the time that I had been in Nazareth House. She had become a long forgotten memory.

I was taken into the washroom and plonked up on the shelf between the wash basins. Elizabeth was already there and Sister Mary was wiping her face with a flannel.

"Oh there you are," she said. "Hurry up and get her ready Kathleen. Mrs. Traynor has been waiting a long time."

Clean socks were put on my feet and my face was rubbed over with a coarse flannel that left my cheeks stinging. And my hair was combed until it hurt, but I was too stunned to protest.

Scrubbed and polished, we were taken down the long passage to the parlour.

"You are going to meet your mother," Sister Mary said. "Be on your best behaviour."

In the parlour we waited outside the visitors room.

There was the old familiar smell of wax polish. And after all these years, the portrait of the Pope was still hanging there on the wall.

"I will go in first and tell your mother that you are here," Sister Mary said. She knocked on the door and entered the room.

Elizabeth and I looked at each other. "Our mother's here," I whispered. I could hardly believe it. We had a mother and she had come to see us. After a few minutes, the door opened and Sister Mary came out.

"In you go now girls and meet your mother."

She had been sitting down but got up when we entered the room. A tall woman with auburn hair, rouge cheeks, red lips, and intense piercing blue eyes. The brown fur coat that she was wearing came down to her ankles just above her high heel shoes.

There was a strong scent that permeated the room. It was much better than the smell of wax polish.

"Hello. Do you know who I am?" she asked.

I just stood there entranced.

"I'm your mother," she said.

She spoke differently than Elizabeth and I, or anyone else in Nazareth House. It wasn't apparent to us at that time but she had a broad Scottish accent.

"What do you think of your girls then, Mrs. Traynor?" Sister Mary asked.

"They have grown up so much, I hardly recognise them," she said, closely scrutinising us.

"Elizabeth is a lot like you, Mrs. Traynor."

"Yes, she has taken after me with her colouring," she said, admiring my sister's wavy auburn hair which had been allowed to hang loose over her shoulders.

I'd been forced to have my head shaved because of the ringworm infection. It was still growing back but it was darker and not as curly as before. Sister Mary explained why I'd had my head shaved. Mother seemed concerned.

"I will leave you then," Sister Mary said.

"Just ring the bell when you are ready to leave, Mrs. Traynor."

"Thank you sister, I will."

45

I must have been feeling left out, as this lady had seemed more interested in Elizabeth. When Sister Mary had left the room, I said to this stranger, "You are MY mother aren't you?"

"Of course I am." She was astonished.

"Why do you ask?" she enquired.

"Elizabeth has your hair," I said.

She laughed.

"That's because she has taken after the Waldies. You have taken after your father. You look just like him, and I don't mean that miserable old Raphy," she said.

I was too young to fully understand the implication of her words.

She looked at us both intensely, as if not quite believing that we belonged to her. And the feeling was mutual.

"I have a present for you," she said to me.

Out of a large brown paper bag, she produced a doll.

It was three feet tall and made of soft material. It was dressed like one of those French Can Can girls. It was wearing a scarlet dress, black stockings, garters, suspenders, high heels, frilly pantaloons and a bra. It had long black hair, a painted face with brown eyes, red lips and cheeks. The nuns would not have approved.

"Dressed up like a brazen hussy," Sister Wulstan would have said.

When our mother left, Sister Mary put the doll on top of the cupboard, "Just to keep it safe."

It soon disappeared. I never saw it again.

Elizabeth and I were elated after her visit, and she had arranged with the nuns to take us out for a day the following week. We had a mother! It was so important to have one of those when you were in Nazareth House. It gave you hope that one day you would be freed. The other girls were envious.

"You will soon be out of this prison," Mari said. "I'm jealous."

No one ever visited her and she knew nothing about her family background.

The following week, Mother turned up in all her finery – fur coat, gloves and big hat. She was always elegantly dressed. There would have been those who thought she had quite a nerve, because the nuns who went out begging door to door for charitable handouts were keeping us, her children.

For the next few months, she proudly paraded us around her old friends in Middlesbrough. Elizabeth and I were taken to a council estate and introduced to Nora, whom she said was a good friend of hers.

They used to visit the pubs in the 'Boro when Mother lived in the area.

"We've had some good times, haven't we May," she said, with a cigarette dangling from her lips.

She had rollers in her hair and a chiffon scarf tied around her head. Her face was lined with wrinkles which made her look weary and probably older than she was. She had a raucous laugh though which was infectious, but it would always end in a fit of coughing.

"Ee May, what bonnie lasses you have.

"That one must be Tommy's?" she said, pointing at me.

"She's the spit of him. And you must be Elizabeth?" she

said to my sister, who nodded shyly.

"She's got your colouring May, hasn't she?"

"Yes, she certainly has."

"Sit here ducks," she said, clearing the newspapers from the sofa.

"Come and sit down while I put the kettle on."

Elizabeth and I sat down and Mother followed Nora into the kitchen.

We sat there wide-eyed, looking around the room. It was the first time that I had been in a small sitting room.

A coal fire was burning in the hearth. On the wall above the fireplace was a clock with a pendulum swinging underneath. There were ornaments on the mantelpiece, on the window ledge, and on the hearth itself. The ashtrays were overflowing and there was a strong smell of tobacco. The settee that we were sitting on smelled foisty. It was such a contrast to the clean antiseptic world of Nazareth House. And I loved it.

Mother came into the room carrying two cups of tea and set them down on the grubby table near to me.

"This will warm you up."

"Do they want any biccies, May?" Nora called from the kitchen.

"Yes please," I whispered to Mother. I was feeling hungry

"I've got some Jammie Dodgers, would you like some?"

Elizabeth was too shy to reply, so I answered for both of us.

"Oooh, yes please."

Nora came in to the room with a packet of biscuits.

"We've never had them before," I said.

"Don't you get biccies in Nazzie House?"

"No."

"Bloody hell, it must seem like Lent every day in that place."

Nora was funny! The way she talked made me giggle.

"Here, have one chick." She offered them around.

"Go on, take two. I don't mind."

We were too polite to take more than one, although I would have liked two. I'd never had Jammie Dodgers before.

Nora and our mother had a good laugh, reminiscing about the good old times. I sat there half-listening to their conversation while basking in the heat and watching the flames flickering in the grate. I'd never seen a coal fire before.

In spite of the squalor, it was comfortable. So this is what a real home looks like. I was envious of the outside kids.

All too soon it was time to go back to Nazareth House. Nora gave us our coats and Elizabeth and I said, "Thank you."

"Ee, such, polite lasses," Nora repeated.

It was getting dark as we headed for the bus, and it was bitterly cold. Waiting at the bus stop, I put my hands in my coat pockets. Nora had put a couple of Jammie Dodgers in each one. And she had done the same for Elizabeth.

"She's kind," I said.

"Yes. Nora's as daft as a brush," Mother replied.

CHAPTER 8

My First Confession

We looked forward to making our first Holy Communion. This would happen around the age of seven, and we would attend Mass looking like little brides in our white dresses and veils. There was a special breakfast laid on after the service, and we would be treated like royalty for a day. We could not receive our first Holy Communion though until we had made our first confession.

I was a pupil at St Mary's Primary School in Middlesbrough. Next door was the old cathedral, and it was here where I made my first confession and subsequently my first Holy Communion. This magnificent building was built in 1878 by Irish immigrants who had come to work in the local industries. I was five years of age when I first stepped inside its huge wooden doors and I was left awestruck. The aisle which led to the high altar stretched way into the distance. Tall grey arches stood on either side of the aisle, and from a lofty height a huge crucifix hung from dark wooden beams. It made me dizzy looking up at it. I often wondered what would happen if it fell on the worshippers below.

The altarpiece was adorned with colourful paintings and statuettes of the apostles and saints. These wonderful icons were a welcome distraction from the long monotonous services that we children had to endure.

We rehearsed in the classroom for our first confession. And we practiced what we had to say. We were to start with: "Bless me Father for I have sinned." This would be followed by the confessing of sins. The priest would give you a penance in the form of prayers, then you made an act of contrition. Having made your first confession, you were then allowed to make your first Holy Communion. This is what we really wanted.

A few weeks beforehand, we were taken to look around the confessionals. They were situated towards the back of the cathedral. There were two doors on either side of the confessional boxes. One was the priest's entrance, which was out of bounds to us. The other door was for the confessor.

"You may have a look inside," our teacher, Miss Murray, said.

The old wooden door creaked loudly as we opened it. It was dark and dank inside, and there was a stale musty smell. It was very scary.

The day came for me to make my first confession. I, along with other anxious girls, sat in a pew waiting our turn to enter the confessional box.

At last it was my turn. I went across to the confessional box and opened the door. There was a dim light on the priest's side. I remembered to close the door so that only the priest could hear my confession.

In the semi-darkness, I almost stumbled over the kneeler and put my hand on the cold damp wall to steady myself. I knelt down and heard a scraping sound. The grille opened and the priest's face appeared. I made the sign of the cross and opened with the words that we had rehearsed so many times: "Bless me father for I have sinned. This is my first confession."

I was nervous. What sins had I to confess? There was an eerie silence as I knelt there in semi- darkness. He was waiting for me to say something. The teachers had talked about the different types of sins.

Telling lies was only a venial sin, they'd said. It was less serious than murder, which was a mortal sin. I racked my brains. Had I told any lies? What if I say I have when I haven't? But that would be a lie wouldn't it? I was confused.

I hadn't murdered anyone, although I'd felt like doing so when that bully Cowan had picked on me. Was that a sin? I'd better not tell him that. Just think of the penance he'd give me.

It seemed ages before a voice eventually said, "Have you been naughty?"

"No!" I burst out indignantly.

There was silence. The hard wooden kneeler was hurting my knees. But I didn't dare move. After a few moments he spoke again.

"Well then, say one Hail Mary for your penance. And make an act of contrition."

I mumbled through the words of contrition I had remembered, and after receiving a blessing I got up and made my way out of the door. I was so relieved that it was over.

Jeannie followed me into the confessional and was not so fortunate. She had been too frightened to close the door and her confession could be heard by all. There were lots of giggling amongst the girls and one of the teachers, frustrated that this solemn service was turning into a farce, got up and closed the door to the confessional. An almighty scream was heard, followed by a fumbling of the door knob and a very frightened Jeannie came out. "I-I'm n-not g-going back i-in t-there," she said.

The priest came out of his side of the confessional, and he was livid!

"What is all the commotion about?" he asked angrily.

He turned to the children still waiting to make their confessions.

"This is God's house," he barked. "Perhaps you should add talking in church to your list of sins." And he went back into the confessional, slamming the door shut behind him.

I felt for those girls who had yet to make their confession. What penance would the priest give them? Maybe they would have to say the whole five decades of the Rosary.

CHAPTER 9

School

The school that we Nazareth House girls attended when we left Saint Mary's Primary School was Saint Richard's Secondary Modern. It catered for both boys and girls but we were kept apart by a six-foot dividing wall. There was no contact with the boys at school, but you would see them on their way to and from the school.

There was a headmaster for the boys' side and a headmistress for us girls.

The girls' headmistress was called Mother Philippa. She was from an order of nuns called the Faithful Companions of Jesus and she lived in the Newlands convent in Middlesbrough.

She was obviously well educated but quite mad, we thought. She was the only nun amongst an all-female teaching staff.

On the last day of each term in her posh accent, she would remind us that in order to have a good holiday we should put God first, others second and self last.

Mother Philippa had a long oval face and bags under her eyes, which made her look permanently tired. I thought that it was because of all the reading that she did. If we went into her room she would be sitting at a large table that was overloaded with paperwork. And the bookcases on either side of her room were crammed with books. She was always busy and trying to do half-a-dozen things at once, and would often ask you questions but not always wait for an answer.

Her mouth would open wide with surprise, especially if she was told that any of the Nazareth House girls had been misbehaving. We were expected to be on our best behaviour at all times and set a good example to others. It was difficult as school was our little bit of freedom. We were mixing with the 'outside' girls and learning so much more about the world than we could ever get in the home.

Mother Philippa enjoyed gardening and kept a well-manicured lawn at the front of the school, and we would help plant her favourite flowers in the borders. She may have been busy but she always took time to admire the flowers and plants. Some of the classrooms overlooked the garden, and if she happened to glance out of the window during a lesson she would stop in mid-sentence to comment: "The crocus vernus have arrived," or "The convallaria majalis is blossoming."

She called the plants by their Latin names, so we were not always sure which one of them she would be talking about.

"Is that the Lily of the Valley?" we would ask.

Or, if we really didn't know: "Is that the white or the red one, Mother Philippa?"

She did try to get us to take an interest in plants and flowers, but many of the girls came from homes with only a backyard.

And we didn't do gardening at Nazareth House.

Mother Philippa was not as strict as the nuns in the

orphanage. I only recall being punished by her once.

There was a new teacher, a Miss Dawson, who had joined the school at the start of the term. It was her first teaching post and we in her class made the most of her inability to control us. She was slim and dark-haired with brown puppy-dog eyes, and she had a pointed chin which she would stroke if she were worried or tense (and this was often). We used to copy her doing this, but she either pretended she hadn't noticed or if she had chose to ignore us.

One very cold morning in January, we were in the playground and she was blowing the whistle then shouting, "Come on girls, please line up or we will be late for assembly."

Most of us carried on talking among ourselves. I was engrossed in listening to a conversation that Pauline Byrne was having with Noreen Clark.

She was recalling a conversation her mam had had with her aunty.

"Me mam says that she can't afford to have any more kids, she's got six mouths to feed already.

"And me Aunty Sheila says to her: 'Catholic or no Catholic, he should tie a knot in it'."

I remember being curious about what 'it' was, but I never got the chance to ask. Whack! I felt a stinging pain right across the back of my legs. I turned round. It was Mother Philippa and she was holding a large cane in her hand. She went on to the next girl and the next, lashing out on exposed legs.

"Ouch! Ouch!" the girls cried as they were hit on the

legs with the cane. We were wearing short socks, and as it was such a cold day it intensified the pain

"How dare you disobey Miss Dawson," she screeched. "How dare you."

I had never seen her so angry.

The girls scarpered in all directions.

Miss Dawson just stood there, a worried look on her face and stroking her chin.

I was left with a large welt on the back of my legs for the rest of the day. It was no good complaining like some of the girls did when they got home. You would have had been given further punishment had you complained to the nuns.

I was mad at myself afterwards because I quite liked Mother Philippa and I know that she saw me as one of the girls that she could depend on, so I felt that I had let her down. (We Catholics tend to have a guilt complex – it's all that talk of martyrdom.)

This episode did not stop Mother Philippa from making me prefect. One of my duties was to inform on all latecomers. I had to wait at the entrance to the school and write down the names of those girls who had arrived after nine o'clock. They would be punished by having to stay back after school and write lines.

I was a sucker for a sob story, or rather for a bar of Highland Toffee. There were girls who were regularly late for school and you would get the same explanations.

"Sorry I'm late," Noreen Clark would say. "I had to take me little sister to the infants' school."

I would feel sorry for her.

"You will have to sneak into the cloakroom," I said. "And if anyone catches you, say that you weren't late but had left your hankie in your coat pocket." (Encouraging others to lie – that's only a venial sin.)

"Ah thanks Anne, you're my favourite prefect."

"Me mam slept in 'cos the clock's broken," whined Mona Walsh, rubbing her eyes and shoving her unkempt hair back from her forehead.

"All right, I'll let you off this time," I would say for the umpteenth time.

Marlene Walker would just saunter through the door

"I know I'm late, but I stopped at the shop to buy you this."

What could I say? A bar of Highland Toffee was a rare treat for me.

Mother Philippa must have thought that I had a good influence on the girls because when I was on duty there weren't many latecomers.

Little did she know.

There were some really nice 'outside' girls that were in my class. They felt sorry for me for being in the orphanage, but I didn't want to be singled out or pitied. I just wanted to fit in.

A girl called Margaret O'Neill wanted to adopt me. My best friend was Diana Burke. She was pretty with dark curly hair. One day Diana said that she would be having fish and chips for lunch. I was envious as we never got them in the home. She invited me round to her house. I sneaked out of school at the lunch break.

When we arrived at her home, her four siblings were sat

around the table. "I've got five mouths to feed already," her mother said, but she told me to sit down and we all shared the fish and chips that had come wrapped in newspaper. They were delicious and I had my first taste of vinegar.

Unfortunately, one of the girls from the home who had not been invited told Sister Mary. I was ordered to scrub the scullery floor for a week and was not allowed to go to Diana's house again. But it was worth it.

I enjoyed sports at school and was quite competitive. I was in the netball team and was a shooter. There were four teams at the school. These were Nazareth, Fatima, Rome and Montmatre. Each team was represented by a different colour. These were green, blue, yellow and red. You would be assigned to a team on your first day at school and would have to remain with it until the day you left.

I was chosen to be in the Nazareth team. I was given a green badge to pin to my tunic and I would have to wear a green band over my shoulder when I played netball.

Nazareth would not have been my choice. The name was too close to home. I would have preferred to have been in Montmatre as it sounded rather grand. And, besides, red was my favourite colour then.

A teacher was chosen to be the leader of each team. They were just as competitive against each other. You could collect points for your team throughout the term for either good behaviour, schoolwork and for collecting the most money for the missionary babies. At the end of each term there would be a netball tournament between the four teams and the winners would receive a cup.

The best thing, though, was that Mother Philippa gave

everyone a piece of her home-made fudge which she had baked herself in the convent. It was delicious!

I also enjoyed playing hockey. There was always lots of competition between the outside girls and the 'Nazzie House kids' as we were called. This is when we got our own back for the name-calling that we endured throughout the term.

There would be us girls in one team opposing some of the 'outside' girls. When we would bully off it would be one, two, three- whack on the opposing girl's ankle. The teacher was never close enough to see it, and if she had we would have said that it was an accident. We would be off up the field and the other team would be hollering after us. But, we didn't stop and we won quite often. It was our way of levelling the score.

There were three teachers that had an effect on me at the time. One was the science teacher, Miss Reed. She was a strange woman. Her hair was grey and severely tied back in a bun, and she wore a long grey dress and overcoat which reached down to her ankles. She wore matching grey shoes and stockings. Her attire you would say was Victorian, very old-fashioned! Her eyes were light, maybe they were grey as well, and she had a tight mouth that didn't open much. And when she did speak it was in a dull monotonous tone.

"Gals, get out your pans and pancils out from your desk." That is what it sounded like as she seemed to speak through gritted teeth.

I did enjoy her lessons though. I found science to be an interesting subject and in one test I did exceptionally well.

I had taken my science book back to Nazareth House to revise. I would have been in trouble if I'd been caught as you weren't allowed to take your school books home. I revised as best as I could while doing my daily chores.

It was worth it though. I came out on top with 95%. The year above had also been given the same test as our class. So overall I was the winner.

Miss Reed must have been impressed because she gave me a gold star.

I put the test paper on my desk so all could see the gold star. My face was flushed with pride.

"Did you get a gold star?" I was asked repeatedly as my classmates passed my desk.

"Yes," I said proudly

I was called 'Clever Clogs,' but I just smiled. This 'Nazzie House' girl had done well!

You couldn't brag for too long though or you would have been seen as a big-head and be ostracised by the other girls. I shrugged it off.

"Wish I was as good at mathematics," I'd say.

The following Monday morning we were having assembly. Mother Philippa, after saying the usual prayers, announced that she had received some good news about one of the girls.

Up to this point I hadn't been taking much notice. I had too many other things on my mind as usual and would spend most of the assembly day-dreaming.

"Miss Reed is very pleased with one of the girls in her class," she said.

Is she talking about me? I wondered.

"She feels that this girl should be rewarded for her efforts."

Rewarded? She had my full attention now.

"This girl is the only one out of both first and second year to score almost one-hundred per cent in the science test. Isn't that a wonderful achievement?"

I became aware that girls were looking at me and whispering my name.

"Bet it's her," they said.

Of course it was me, hadn't they seen my gold star? I mustn't get too big-headed though, so I pretended that I hadn't heard.

Then Mother Philippa shouted:

"Could Anne Traynor come out to the front please?"

I froze. Now, if there is one thing that I dreaded, it was to be hauled out in front of everybody. In Nazareth House that only happened to you if you had done something wrong and the nuns wanted to humiliate you. I didn't move.

"Anne Traynor, where is she?" Mother Philippa asked, narrowing her eyes as she looked around the hall.

"She's here, she's here." Fingers were pointing at me.

"Go on, Mother Philippa wants you." I was shoved from behind.

Reluctantly, I pushed through the throng of girls who turned and stared at me as I made my way to the front. I could hear the comments.

"She's a 'Nazzie House' girl" and "Teacher's pet."

"Oh there you are. Come on up here and stand beside me," Mother Philippa said.

I didn't enjoy this one bit. My face was red and I knew

that I would be teased and called names and, worst of all, be known as Miss Reed's 'pet'. "Well done!" Mother Philippa said.

"And as a reward for your hard work, Miss Reed has suggested that we choose you to go on a free trip to Lourdes."

Miss Reed looked at me and for the first time ever I saw her smile. I felt giddy and light-headed. Standing up there in front of the whole school, all eyes were on me. I did not feel like a winner at all.

Miss Ellis was the mathematics teacher. I disliked her and the feeling was mutual. She resented some of the Nazareth House girls because in her opinion we were being 'kept' by the charity of the nuns and the parish.

"Some parents do not always shirk their responsibilities," she said in answer to one girl's question as to why some Nazareth House girls were in an orphanage when they still had parents. Why we ever got to talk about this in her lesson is a mystery.

The suit that she wore looked more like a uniform. It made you wonder if she had served in the armed forces. She was always in dark clothes, either navy-blue, dark-grey or black, and she wore black laced-up shoes. She had a stocky build with short straight grey hair that was worn in a pageboy style. Her dark brown eyes would peer at you behind half-rimmed glasses.

"Yes, what do you want?" she would sneer at you if you approached her desk. This was something I rarely did, as she seemed to take pleasure in humiliating you.

She had chastised Thelma, one of the Nazareth House

girls, in front of the class for having a 'tide' mark on her neck. The outside girls could have complained to their parents. But we had no person in authority to stick up for us. It was the price you paid for being in an orphanage.

Mother Philippa gave me responsibilities and was fair and Miss Reed did appreciate my efforts in science, but Miss Ellis made me feel stupid.

In her lessons I would waste my time doodling or looking out of the window. I was totally turned off mathematics. I hated the subject. Most of the time she would just ignore us 'stupid' girls and we were placed at the back of the class. On the odd occasion when she did venture to the back of the class to look at our work, she would comment, "What do you expect?"

My end–of-term maths exam results were appalling.

One day, on my way out of her lesson, she told me to wait at her desk. When all the girls had left the classroom she asked: "Why do YOU think that you deserve to go on a free trip to Lourdes?"

I was taken aback by the vicious tone in her voice. I mumbled something about Miss Reed being pleased with my science results.

I wished that I could have been more assertive in her presence. I wanted to say so many things. It's not my fault I'm in Nazareth House. I didn't choose my parents. I didn't ask to be born. Why shouldn't I go on a free trip to Lourdes? Instead, I just stood there feeling guilty that I may be taking the place of some girl more worthy than I. You would have been punished for answering back in the home and this had undermined my confidence.

There was a knock on the door and Mrs. Gethin entered. She was a colleague of Miss Ellis and also a good friend. They went on holidays abroad together. Mrs. Gethin was in her forties and married with no children.

"Tea's made, Miss Ellis."

"I won't be long," she replied.

"What do you think of this girl being given a free trip to Lourdes?" Miss Ellis asked.

"It will be a wonderful experience for her," Mrs. Gethin said, smiling at me.

"Miss Reed is pleased with her results in the science test."

"I do not think that is fair," Miss Ellis said.

"Why?" Mrs. Gethin asked, with a puzzled look on her face.

"Well her mathematics results are a disgrace."

"Are they really?"

I could feel my anger rising. I wanted to say: "It's because I hate maths. And I hate you as well."

"There are other girls more deserving. But their hard-working parents can't afford it."

"I don't want to go."

The words blurted out of my mouth before I could stop them.

"You don't want to go to Lourdes?" Mrs. Gethin asked.

She seemed as shocked at my outburst as I was.

"No," I said defiantly.

"But this is a golden opportunity to visit the grotto of Our Blessed Virgin. It is a wonderful experience."

She looked at Miss Ellis for support but there was none forthcoming.

"It's a place where miracles are performed and Miss Ellis and I go every year."

If she wanted me to change my mind she had blown it. Now I definitely did not want to go. I remained silent.

Miss Ellis tutted.

"That's gratitude for you. I suppose I had better inform Mother Philippa."

And with a look of triumph on her face she and Mrs. Gethin left the room.

I stood there utterly deflated.

You idiot, I thought.

I never did go to Lourdes.

The geography teacher was Mrs. Rotini. She was young and pretty. She had met an Italian on holiday in Rome had fallen in love and now they were married.

She had dark curly hair, big green eyes and a smile that lit up her face.

With her matching red lipstick and nail polish and flowery dress, she looked like a Fifties film star.

I enjoyed her lessons. She would get us to choose a country from our atlas and then we had to write about its people and customs.

While we were doing this, she would sit at her desk stroking her hair and gazing out of the window day-dreaming: her legs crossed and one slip-on shoe would be dangling from her foot.

We loved listening to her talking Italian. After school had ended her handsome husband would come and pick her up on his moped. We would be staring out of the window.

"Ah! Isn't he gorgeous?" we'd crow. We all wanted an Italian husband.

Mrs. Rotini was kind and I did all right in my geography exams. Nowhere near the top of the class though, because I would spend my time daydreaming too.

CHAPTER 10

The School Play

Mother Philippa taught religious knowledge and English literature. She adored William Shakespeare and tried to educate us into appreciating his works.

We were a school where quite a few of the children would be described today as coming from a socially deprived background. We were not well read and those kinds of books were not top of the list for us. Undeterred, one year for our Christmas play she decided to put on Twelfth Night by William Shakespeare.

Mother Philippa would choose the brighter academic girls from the fourth year to take on the main roles. Then she would look for volunteers throughout the school to play the minor parts.

I was twelve-years-old and in my second year at the school. Nobody in our class was volunteering. It was all right to just walk on stage and be an extra in a scene, but to actually speak in that weird language? No way!

One day we were having an English lesson and we were on tenterhooks as to who was going to be chosen for the school play. Mother Philippa was desperately looking for girls to fill the minor roles.

"Come along girls, who would like the privilege of taking part in this delightful play by William Shakespeare?" Mother Philippa said cheerfully. I was trying to keep my head down, hoping that she wouldn't notice me. But I had been at the school for over a year now and she knew me quite well, as I would run errands for her.

I couldn't hide either as I was wearing the Nazareth House uniform. We girls were compliant and obedient. We had to be – if we were reported to the nuns in Nazareth House for bad behaviour we would be in BIG trouble.

I was waiting for her to call my name. It came soon enough.

"Anne, would you like to play the part of the Sea Captain?" I wasn't used to being asked if I wanted to do something. In Nazareth House the nuns told you what to do. You had no choice in the matter. I was stumped. I wanted to say, "No Mother Philippa, not really. I blush too easily. I'll forget my lines, and I think that Shakespeare waffles on too much." Instead, I went red in the face and made some incoherent remark which she took to mean yes.

"Wonderful!" she said.

"Anne will take the part of the Sea Captain."

"Whom shall we choose to play the part of the Arresting Officer?" she said, tapping on her desk and looking around the room.

There was a lot of uncomfortable shuffling and girls mumbling, "I don't want to do it."

Well, I've already got a part to play so she can't pick on me, I thought. I copied what the other girls were doing and I looked around the class waiting for a hand to be raised.

"Marlene, wouldn't you like to take on this role?"

"I can't, Mother Philippa, I get tongue tied," she said.

Marlene gets tongue tied? You must be kidding, I

thought. She never shuts up.

There were other excuses from other girls and Mother Philippa was getting impatient. Exasperated, she turned to me.

"Anne, it's only a small part so you could take on the part of the Officer as well as the Sea Captain," she said. And she didn't wait for a reply.

That is how I came to take part in my very first play and I had to take on two roles.

I had only a few weeks to learn the lines of both the Sea Captain and the Officer. They were minor roles but I really did not want to take part in this play. At rehearsals I felt shy and awkward and Mother Philippa was forever telling me to put more feeling into the words. It didn't help that Mari and Marlene were sat in the front seats, mimicking my every word. I felt silly and being sensitive I blushed easily. Eventually, Mother Philippa got annoyed with the distractions and ordered them out of rehearsals.

When Mother Philippa was not available (and this was often) Donna Martin was put in charge of rehearsals.

She was quite amiable and I grumbled to her about the concerns I had remembering my lines, and the silly clothes I would have to wear. I was hoping that she would agree to take on the role of the Sea Captain, as she was the understudy. But she refused. I asked her if I could alter the words of one of the Captain's speeches as it was quite long winded.

"What! Change the words? Mother Philippa would have a fit," she said.

We went through the scene where the Sea Captain

meets Viola for the first time. Donna took on Viola's role.

The Captain's last lines in the scene are: "Be you his eunuch, and your mute I'll be: When my tongue blabs, then let mine eyes not see."

"What's a eunuch?"

"Dunno, I've never heard of it," Donna said.

"Mother Philippa says that I have got to get an understanding of the words. Well then, how am I supposed to put more feeling into it if I don't know what I'm talking about?" I said. (I was just being petty. I did not want to be in this play.)

"You will have to ask Mother Philippa – that's if you can get hold of her."

I didn't think anymore about it until a few evenings later, when I was in the sewing room with Sister Agnes. We were darning socks. She asked me how I was getting on at school. I told her about the school play and I thought this would be a good time to ask her a question. It turned into quite a confusing conversation.

"Sister Agnes," I said, "what is a eunuch?"

"A what?"

"A eunuch."

"How do you spell that?"

"E-u-n-u-c-h. I'm in the school play and in one of my lines I have to say: 'Be you his eunuch'."

"What play is that?"

"It's called Twelfth Night and Mother Philippa has chosen it for our Christmas play."

Sister Agnes looked puzzled. She thought for a moment. "Twelfth Night? I've never heard of that play. Is it something to do with the twelve days of Christmas?"

"I don't think it's got anything to do with Christmas."

"What is it about?"

I gave her a shortened version of my scene.

"Well, there is this girl called Viola and she has a twin brother called Sebastian. They are at sea and the boat that they are in overturns. Viola is rescued but she thinks that her brother has drowned.

"But, I'm the Sea Captain and I tell her that I may have seen him clinging to a mast.

"I say to her, 'Be you his eunuch,' whatever that means. Then she goes and dresses up as a boy."

"Why would she do that?" Sister Agnes asked.

"Well, Donna Martin says that it's because women on their own were not safe from men."

"Who is this Donna Martin? She sounds like a sensible girl."

"She is one of the 'outside girls' Sister, and she helps us rehearse.

"Do you know Sister, Donna says that all the women's roles were played by men in them days."

"How very odd," Sister Agnes said, shaking her head.

"Donna says that in those days when they put on a nativity play at Christmas, Mary would have been played by a man."

Sister Agnes was aghast.

"That can't be true," she said. "Surely they must have made exceptions for Mary the Blessed Virgin. After all, she is the Mother of Jesus.

"Where does Donna Martin get her information from anyway?"

"Mother Philippa, I think."

Sister Agnes looked shocked. She was speechless.

I was taken aback by her reaction. I was only relating what Donna had told me.

She carried on darning a sock, then she enquired:

"What happens to this Viola, who's pretending to be a boy?"

"Lady Olivia falls in love with her."

"This Lady Olivia, is she in disguise as well."

"What do you mean Sister, is she in disguise?"

I wasn't sure if she was asking me if Lady Olivier was really a man pretending to be a woman (like Viola had taken on the disguise of a male) or if it was a male taking on a female role. I decided it was the latter.

"It's not a lad playing the part of Lady Olivier, Sister Agnes. It's Barbara Brennan, she's our head girl. And Lady Olivier's a woman and she wanted nothing to do with men," I added. I'd read that somewhere.

"But how then does she meet this Viola, who's supposed to be a boy?" Sister Agnes asked.

"Lady Olivia is told that he's handsome and he won't go away until he has met with her. So she agrees to meet him."

"She soon changed her mind. But would she not think that Viola was a girl's name?"

"No because," (then I remembered) "she's changed her name to Cesario."

Sister Agnes stopped darning the socks. "Would you not think you'd get confused with the changes?"

With all the interruptions I was getting confused myself.

"But Viola – or is it Cesario," I said (I'd forgotten which

one) "has really come to see Lady Olivia, to get her to fall in love with Orsino."

"Orsino, now is he a man?"

"Yes Sister, he's a Duke."

"He'll have plenty of money then."

"Yes, but Lady Olivia really loves Viola," I said.

"Does she now?"

"But Cesario fancies Orsino."

"Does he now?" Sister Agnes looked perplexed.

"Does Orsino know that Cesario is really a woman called Viola?"

"Oh no, he thinks that he is a young man and he is very fond of him."

"Is he now?" Sister Agnes frowned.

"It's got a happy ending, Sister Agnes."

"It has? I think that you will have to ask one of the teachers about whatever you needed to know. Mother Philippa likes these sorts of plays then, does she?"

"Yes Sister, she loves them."

"God bless us and save us."

I didn't get round to asking any of the teachers. I had asked some of the girls if they could find out what a eunuch was, but nobody seemed that interested. Until one day out of curiosity Mari had asked a teacher and had been told to 'wash her mouth out'. Now that was a red rag to a bull for Mari.

One afternoon after our last rehearsal I was coming down the steps at the back of the stage. I was surprised to see Mari and Marlene waiting for me. Marlene was smirking

"Shall we tell her?" she said to Mari.

"What's so funny? Did I fluff my lines?" I asked.

"We know what a eunuch is."

Mari whispered in my ear as if she was telling me a dirty secret.

"It's a man who has been castrated."

I didn't understand. "What does castrated mean? And how did you find out?"

"That clever clogs Pearl looked it up in her dictionary. And Marlene's dad says that if Joseph Connor doesn't stop hanging round their Patsy then he will castrate him. So it has something to do with lads."

"Let's have a look in the book, Pearl," Marlene shouted.

Pearl came over looking slightly flustered. She handed the dictionary to Marlene. "It's there on the right," she said.

"What does it mean?" I asked

"You have a look," Pearl said.

We huddled over the book and read. A eunuch is a man who has had his testicles removed.

I had never seen a naked man before – only a statue of one when we were at a museum and we'd been told not to look. So I wasn't really sure what part of a man's anatomy had been 'removed'.

"So a eunuch is a man, who has had all his you-know-what removed," Mari giggled.

"Not all of it," Marlene said. "Just…" and she burst out laughing.

"Ooh, it's a sin to talk about a naked man," Mari said. She thought it was hilarious. I was quite concerned. I certainly didn't want to have to go in the confessional box and tell the priest that we had been talking about castrated men.

Marlene wondered if Mother Philippa knew what a eunuch was, after all she was a nun.

"The Bishop is coming to see the play on Friday," giggled Mari. "Make sure you say: 'Be you his eunuch' loud and clear."

We went into fits of laughter.

Then I thought of the conversation I'd had with Sister Agnes.

Maybe she hadn't known either.

I too saw the funny side.

Oh, the sweet innocents that we were!

CHAPTER 11

Rea's Café

It was difficult to get to know Mother, especially as she was always flitting in and out of our lives. We never knew when she was going to come and visit us, as she would turn up unexpectedly. It was only when Elizabeth and I grew up that we got to know and understand the complex person that she was. It was during these visits that we would ask her about the rest of the family.

She had no siblings and her parents were Scottish, and she herself was born in Glasgow. Her father was working as a railway engineer in India, and that is where she had spent her formative years. They had servants to wait on them and Mother had been privately educated in a convent. Raphy was working as a foreman in the same foundry as Grandfather, (Mother chased after him, we were told), and they married in India where Denis was born.

We never knew our grandmother; she died when Denis was five years old and before Elizabeth and I were born.

After the war, they had come to live in Middlesbrough. It was Raphy's home town, and he got a job in the local steelworks.

After a comfortable life in India, Mother found it hard to adjust to a life without servants and other luxuries. It must have been a depressing time for her. But she was also irresponsible and would go out on the town while Raphy was at work, leaving Denis in charge of Elizabeth and me.

Although she had affairs, Raphy would not have given her a divorce as his Catholism forbade it. In future years, on the rare occasion that they met, they would snipe at each other. They blamed one another for the breakdown of their marriage, but the truth was that they were totally mismatched.

There would be periods when Mother would come and visit Elizabeth and I quite regularly at Nazareth House. When we were older we were allowed to visit her at her bedsit in Linthorpe Village, but then she would disappear from the area and we would not see her for months.

She liked a drink. The trouble was if she was out on the town and saw any of the nuns from Nazareth House, she would waylay them and enquire after her daughters Elizabeth and Anne.

The nuns would then talk about her within hearing distance of my sister and I.

"What a disgrace," they would say, "and her having such lovely girls."

Elizabeth would plead with Mother not to talk to the nuns, especially if she had been drinking, but it never bothered Mother in the slightest. She was brazen.

Sometimes, Mother would take Elizabeth and me out in the afternoon. After a walk in Albert Park, we usually ended up in Rea's Café. It was a self-service café and therefore you had to help yourself to cutlery. We would sit at a table with our Bovril and crackers (a treat for us) and Mother with her cup of tea.

One day, she was in a bad mood for some reason and was irritable.

"Where are the teaspoons?" she snapped.

"There weren't any," I replied.

Sighing deeply, she got up and went over to the cutlery box. But there were no teaspoons. She went to the front of the queue, ignoring the customer who was being served, and in her broad Glaswegian accent shouted: "There are no teaspoons. Are we supposed to stir the tea with our fingers? The service here is disgraceful."

Everyone looked at her. Elizabeth and I were mortified.

"I will get you a spoon as soon as I have served this customer madam," said the woman behind the counter, startled at the sudden outburst.

"This is bad service," Mother shouted and demanded to see the manager.

"I am afraid the manageress is unavailable at this moment as she is on her break."

"Well I have got something to say to her when she gets back."

Mother was given a teaspoon and she came over and slammed it down on the table. When she was in this mood I was terrified of her. She could flare up at the least thing, and then things would be thrown about. My sister, aware of the attention she was drawing, tried to calm her down.

"Shh," she said. "Can you keep your voice down? You are showing us up."

Mother went berserk.

"How dare you talk to me like that? Who do you think you are? Wait until the nuns hear how you talked to your mother," she rambled on. We looked at her in amazement.

"I'm only telling you to calm down and stop shouting," Elizabeth said quietly.

The woman who had been serving behind the counter came up to our table.

"Madam, our manageress is here if you wish to complain about the service. And I would like to remind you to please keep your voice down as we have other customers to consider."

"I'm surprised that you have any customers at all," Mother said sarcastically.

She got up and followed the woman to the counter.

"Fancy her making a fuss just because there were no teaspoons," Elizabeth said.

We were very reserved, especially given our upbringing, and didn't like drawing attention to ourselves. Everyone was staring at us.

"What a showing up," Elizabeth said.

Mother came back to the table, obviously not satisfied with seeing the manageress.

"I'm going to write to head office," she said loudly.

"You don't have to take it that far," Elizabeth said, but she instantly regretted having spoken.

Mother was furious and she turned on her.

"I've had enough of your cheek," she shouted. "You are just like Raphy, always whinging. I am taking Anne back to Liverpool with me. And I am leaving you in Nazareth House."

I stayed with Mother for a week in the summer holidays. I didn't really want to go without my sister.

Elizabeth came to the railway station to see us off. She

waved as the train pulled away. "I wish that she was coming with us now," Mother said. But that was Mother – she was quick tempered and would say things that she'd regret but be too stubborn or proud to admit that she was wrong.

We arrived at Liverpool's bustling Lime Street Station. Then we got the bus to Wavertree where Mother rented a flat in a house in Botanic Road. It was on the second floor and overlooked Wavertree Park.

We had no sooner put our cases down when there was a knock on the door. It was Mother's Dutch boyfriend, Tony. Elizabeth and I had met him when she was living in Middlesbrough. He was a merchant seaman and when his ship had moved to Liverpool, Mother had followed.

I was disappointed as I was looking forward to spending a pleasant week with Mother and getting to know her better.

It didn't help that a few hours later she went out with him for a 'few drinks' and left me alone in the flat. Later, I laid there on the sofa which was to be my bed with the glow from the street lamp lighting up the room. I'd switched the light off to save electricity as Mother had to constantly feed the meter to keep it on.

Mother arrived home after the pubs had closed. She was merry and laughing and joking with Tony. "Elizabeth would not approve," she said.

I missed my sister and wished that she had been here. She was not afraid to stand up to Mother and was very protected of me. She'd be annoyed that Mother had gone out and left me on my own.

After only a few days, I was homesick and I wanted to

go back to Nazareth House. The girls from the orphanage would be at Redcar now having a great time on the beach and I was miserable.

"You must be mad wanting to come back to Nazzie House," Mari would have said.

I told Mother and she telephoned the Mother Superior at Nazareth House and was told that I could return early if I wished. However, soon after, I made friends with a young couple who had a little boy. They lived a few doors away from Mother. They were staying with the husband's parents and his family. Mother got on well with the grandparents.

The family welcomed me into their home and I spent most of the days at their house, listening to the latest songs. I went out on day-trips to the seaside with them. I was allowed to take the little boy out to the park and this cheered me up. This suited Mother too as she was free to go out and about with Tony, invariable ending up in a pub. She warned me not to tell them that I was living in a children's home. I was glad that they never asked, but I'm sure that they must have guessed.

A week later, Mother took me back to the home and soon I was on a train bound for Redcar to spend the rest of the holidays at the seaside resort.

Over the years, during the summer holidays and when Elizabeth and I had reached our teens, the nuns allowed us to visit our mother.

We got on the coach at Middlesbrough Bus Station. It was a long, tedious journey. When we arrived in Liverpool we had to catch a green bus to Wavertree. I remember asking a bus driver if the bus stopped at the Pier head. "I hope so," he said, "otherwise we'll fall in the River Mersey." I loved the Liverpudlian sense of humour.

It was always a struggle for Mother to feed us. In the orphanage we had three regular meals a day. In Mother's house it was either tea and toast or a biscuit. Or she would buy a ham shank from the butcher and make a tasty soup. It was her specialty.

Mother had stomach ulcers which sometimes left her in excruciating pain. She had suffered from them since she was a teenager and had undergone an operation. She would ask for a glass of milk and a biscuit to help relieve the pain when it got really bad. We hated seeing her in pain and Elizabeth and I would try and help out by washing up and cleaning the house.

CHAPTER 12

High Anxiety

I had my first panic attack when I was in my early teens. I was walking down the long passage in the home. It was bustling with the girls making their way to the communal room. We had just come back from the church after the service of Benediction. Suddenly, everything seemed brighter, louder and noisier, and an overwhelming fear came over me.

I tried to push my way to the front but I couldn't get past. I felt trapped and my heart was racing. I thought that I was going to die. The next thing I remember, I was laying on the ground and Christine, one of the senior girls, was by my side.

"Are you all right?" she asked. "Does your head hurt?"

"Why?" I asked weakly.

"You went down with a bump."

I became aware that a group had formed around me. I could hear Sister Wulstan shouting, "What is all this commotion?"

"It's Anne Traynor, Sister. She's laying on the ground. I think that she has fainted and she's banged her head," Christine said.

"Well then, don't stand there gawping. Give her room to breathe. Get away, get away, get away," she snapped, pushing everybody out of the way. She stood over me.

"What are you doing down there, did you fall?" she asked.

"I don't know," I said.

"Well, does anyone know what happened? Was she pushed?"

"I know what happened," Audrey Browne said.

"Me too," Maureen Lang said.

"Well then, will somebody tell me? I haven't got all day."

"She was in front of us and she just started acting strange. I think she's seen a ghost," Audrey Browne said.

"Don't be stupid, there is no such thing as a ghost," Sister Wulstan said scornfully.

"She called out the name of Mary and then she fainted," Maureen said.

"Yes, she did," Angela concurred.

"She'd seen something Sister, honestly," another girl butted in.

Sister Wulstan looked at them and then looked at me. She had a strange expression on her face.

"We had better get her to bed. Can you walk child?" she asked. "Help her up."

Helping hands lifted me to my feet. I was dazed. I was taken upstairs to the dormitory and I lay on my bed. Sister Wulstan sat by my bedside. She ordered one of the girls to fetch a glass of water.

"Do you want anything to eat?" she asked gently.

"No thank you," I replied.

"Tell me what happened?"

I tried to explain. "Everything went bright and I got scared."

"Did our Lady say anything to you?"

"Our Lady?"

"Yes, you called her name. Did you see her?"

I looked at her in astonishment.

I was about to tell her that I hadn't seen anyone when Sister Agnes came into the dormitory.

"The girls told me that Anne fainted after seeing the Blessed Virgin." She looked at me, with her face beaming.

"They said that she went as white as a ghost."

"There is no such thing as a ghost," Sister Wulstan reprimanded her.

"She believes that she may have seen an apparition of the Virgin Mary."

"Holy Mother of God!" Sister Agnes laughed. "Have we a saint in our midst?"

They both looked at me.

I was feeling much better and should have told them there and then.

But I was basking in all the attention. I was seeing a much gentler side to Sister Wulstan.

"We will leave you to rest now," she said as she drew the curtains around my bed.

"You can tell me what Our Lady said in the morning,"

I don't think that she was totally convinced.

There were whisperings among the other girls when they came into the dormitory, and orders had been given that I was not to be disturbed.

Later, lying there in the dark, I started thinking that maybe this wasn't such a good idea. After all, I might be expected to perform miracles. What would Sister Agnes say? "God bless us and save us."

The next morning, Sister Wulstan reprimanded me and Mari for giggling in church. "You of all people," she said, pointing at me.

It was impossible for me to be saintly.

CHAPTER 13

Corpus Christi Procession

There were aspects of the rituals of the Catholic faith that I enjoyed, in particular the pomp and ceremony of the Corpus Christi procession that was held annually on the streets of Middlesbrough.

One year, I was a flower strewer. I wore a long, white satin dress and veil, white shoes, socks and gloves. I also had a blue cape with a red lining draped around my shoulders. I held a golden basket filled with blue and white petals. I felt quite important in my grand attire.

The procession started out from the Old Market Place. It went past the Cathedral and through the town centre and finished at the Newlands Convent. It was about a two-mile walk.

We flower strewers had to take about eight steps and then turn around and scatter the petals on the ground. At the start of the procession I was rather generous and scattered the petals liberally. Then I realised I wasn't going to have enough to last all the way, so I cut it down to one or two.

We still had quite a distance to go when I ran out of petals. Several girls near to me had no petals left either. We weren't sure what to do and looked to each other for guidance.

"Keep going," one girl whispered, as she pretended to

scatter handfuls of imaginary petals. We copied what she was doing. People lining the route were looking at us expecting to see a shower of colourful petals cascading from our hands. Any comments they may have made they kept to themselves, as following close behind was the Bishop of the Diocese carrying the monstrance which held the Blessed Sacrament.

The bishop walked under a canopy which was held aloft by four men wearing dark suits. They were from the Order of the Knights of Saint Columbus. Accompanying them were priests and altar boys who were swinging the thurible.

All the Catholic schools took part in the procession. The girls from the infant schools wore white dresses, shoes and veils and the boys wore immaculate white shirts. The older children wore their school uniform.

The parishioners from the diocese walked behind their own church's banner which usually depicted one of the saints.

Some of the spectators that lined the route took part in the ceremony and prayed and sang hymns along with the walkers.

Others, maybe they were non believers, would stare in amazement at the spectacle.

It was an incredible experience. There were so many people involved that you felt part of a big extended family.

There was also a procession held in Nazareth House during the month of May to honour Our Lady.

The service would start in the church. Then as the procession made its way to the garden, we sang hymns and said the Rosary. At the grotto in the garden, the hymn

"Bring Flowers of the Rarest" would be sung whilst the May Queen placed a floral crown on the head of the statue of Mary.

I was chosen to be the May Queen one year, but it came about by chance. I had to take a message from Sister Mary to Sister Wulstan. She was in the changing room with the girls who were trying on the dresses for the May procession.

The May Queen had not yet been chosen but it was assumed that one of the girls present would have the honour. But apparently the dress that was specially made for a May Queen did not fit any of the girls.

I was about to leave when Sister Wulstan asked me to try on the dress. I was very surprised to be asked as were the other girls. My hair was short, and the girl chosen to be May Queen usually had long hair.

I was puzzled but I put the dress on. It fitted me perfectly. It could have been made for me. I also had to try on some white shoes and I found the perfect pair. I was to be the May Queen! I couldn't believe that this was happening.

It was like a scene from Cinderella. (Only Sister Wulstan didn't look like a Fairy Godmother.)

Four of the girls were chosen to be my train bearers, and on a warm Sunday in the month of May one totally bemused May Queen crowned the statue of Our Lady.

CHAPTER 14

Running Away

I ran away from Nazareth House when I was thirteen. We often talked about running away, but I wasn't as enthusiastic as some of the other girls and besides, nothing ever came of it. That was until a warm July evening, when Sister Mary sent me on an errand. I was to take a note to Sister Carmel, who worked in the sewing room. This meant that I'd have to cross over the yard that separated the children's area from the old folks.

It was six o'clock and there was nobody about, or so I thought, until I turned the corner and almost bumped into Mari.

"What are you doing?" we both said.

"I'm waiting for somebody," Mari replied.

"Who?"

"Can't tell you. It's a secret."

We were not far from the back entrance which led out onto the main road.

"It's not a boy, is it?"

"Don't be daft. How could I sneak a boy in here?"

Someone poked me in the back.

"What are you doing here, Anne Traynor?"

I turned around. It was Katie Foster, and Jeannie was with her. Something was going on.

"What are you up to?" I said.

"Nothing," Katie said unconvincingly.

"Ah, we might as well tell her," said Mari. "She's seen us now."

"Promise you won't tell anyone?"

"No, definitely not. I'm not a tell-tale."

"We are running away."

"What! Running away?"

"Shush!" said Katie. "Someone will hear you."

"Where are you running away to?" I asked

"We are going to Hartlepool. That's where me granny lives," Katie said.

"That's miles away! How are you going to get there?"

"We are going to walk."

"Don't be daft."

"W-We c-could g-get th-the b-bus," said Jeannie.

"Have you any money?" I asked.

"I've saved me pocket money," Katie said smugly.

"You must have been saving all year then," I said sarcastically.

"How many are running away?" I enquired.

"There are just the three of us. Audrey Browne has changed her mind."

"She's chickened out," Katie said.

"She's too scared," Mari added.

"I've told her that if she opens her mouth, I'm going to bash her."

"You kept it quiet about running away," I said to Mari.

"I only just decided."

"When?"

"This morning."

"This morning?"

"Yes. Katie asked me and I said that I'd think about it. But it didn't take me long to make up me mind when old Woolly Bags started yelling at me again."

"You are always in trouble," I laughed.

"Why don't you come with us?" she asked.

"We'll have to go right now," Katie said, who was anxious to get away. "The bell will be going soon for the nuns' vespers, and they'll be locking up. Let's go."

They darted towards the back door. I hesitated; I wasn't sure.

"Hurry up, make up your mind," Mari said, as she opened the door.

If I had thought it over I probably wouldn't have gone. But at that moment it seemed like one big adventure.

"I'm coming," I said, and ran after them. Mari held the door open and soon we were on the outside.

"Which way are we going?" I asked.

"Dunno and I don't care," Mari said.

"I'm just glad to get out of that place."

"We'd better head for the back alley," Katie said. "If anyone is looking out of the windows they'll see us."

We ran down the side street, startling passers-by who quickly moved out of our way. Katie was in the lead, followed by Mari and I with Jeannie trailing behind. We scarpered down one alleyway then another. Eventually we had to stop and wait for Jeannie to catch up. She wanted to rest for a while.

"We have to keep going," Katie insisted.

"We have to get as far away from Nazzie House or we'll get caught."

I was feeling euphoric and giddy. I was running away from Nazareth House. It was absurd! But there was no turning back.

We walked on, my mind was buzzing. I had no idea of where we were going to sleep or what we were going to eat. But it was new and exciting. We had to get onto the main road again and that was risky. I glanced back and, although we had covered quite a distance, I could still see the roof of the orphanage. Suddenly Katie stopped.

"I know what we'll do," she said.

"We'll go on the Transporter. We'll be in Hartlepool in no time."

"How much will it cost?" I asked.

I had no money in my pocket, only a packet of Fruit Pastilles.

Mari and Jeannie said that they didn't have any money on them either.

"My, you planned really well for this running away," I laughed.

"Marlene says that kids don't have to pay," Mari said.

"That Marlene's dead common, I don't like her," Katie said.

"She's too skitty an' all."

"She's alright. She's a good laugh," Mari said.

She was used to being criticized over her friendship with Marlene. It didn't bother her anymore.

"You'll get into trouble hanging around with her," Katie said.

"SHE get me into trouble? Do you not think we're in trouble now?"

We carried on walking, looking back every now and again until at last Nazareth House was out of sight.

"We're free!" Mari shouted.

We arrived at the Albert Bridge and ran down the long wide tunnel, making the Indian war cry with our voices echoing in the darkness. When a train rumbled noisily overhead we dashed to reach the exit.

The Transporter would take us across the water to Port Clarence, and from there we would find our way to Hartlepool via Seaton. The seaside resort of Seaton Carew was familiar to us. The children from the orphanage had been there regularly on bus trips. But Hartlepool? That seemed far away.

"I've never been to Hartlepool," I said to Katie.

"Is it true that they hung a monkey for spying?"

"Nah, me granny says that it's a pack of lies," she replied.

We must have scared Jeannie, who suddenly decided that she would rather stay at Seaton Carew.

We walked briskly and soon we came to the Transporter Bridge.

The Transporter carried cars and passengers in a 'gondola' suspended from the bridge. Those with a less nervous disposition could climb to the top and walk across the bridge from one side to the other.

There was space for cars in the centre of the platform, and there was a closed-in seating area for passengers.

"Don't see any ticket collector," Katie said.

"Let's wait until some people get on. We'll stay close to them," I suggested. "Pretend we're with them."

A young couple came sauntering along, holding hands and chatting. They didn't take any notice of us.

"Let's go," Katie said.

We sneakily followed them into the platform.

"Well, we made it this far," Katie said, optimistically.

The Transporter started to move, slowly at first and then it built up speed.

I saw a man in uniform. We hadn't noticed him coming on board and he was carrying a ticket dispenser.

"That's the ticket collector."

"Ooh, he's coming over," Mari said. "Let's hide."

"I thought you said it was free for kids?" Katie said.

"I was only kidding."

"What!"

"W-we'll g-get th-thrown o-ff," Jeannie cried

"Leave it to me," Mari said.

"That will be one penny each," the ticket collector said, looking at each of us in turn.

"We haven't got any money, Mister. It's my fault, I lost it," Mari said, pretending to cry. "Me dad will play war with me an' all."

We looked at her in amazement. She was so convincing. What an actress! Mother Philippa would have been proud of her. If she could have heard her now she'd have given her a starring role in the school play.

Katie joined in.

"Mister, can you just let us cross? We will pay you on the way back," she pleaded.

"When do you intend to come back?" he asked

Katie was stumped; she blushed. "I dunno," she said.

"Y-you w-wont th-throw u-us o-off, will you?" cried Jeannie.

"No, I couldn't do that," he laughed. Under the peaked hat there was a kindly face.

"Besides, we are already over the water," he said.

I noticed that he was wearing a watch and I asked him the time.

"It's seven o'clock pet," he said.

I'd never been called pet before. It made me smile.

"Is that the time already Mister? Me mam will kill me," Mari whined. She was enjoying this acting lark.

He looked from one anguished face to another.

"Oh, all right then," he said. "But don't be telling everybody. It's more than me job's worth."

"Thank you. Thank you." We thanked him profusely.

"God bless you, Mister," Mari added.

He blushed and smiled as he moved on to collect the fares from the other passengers.

"That was brilliant what you told him, Mari," Katie said.

"I learnt it from Marlene," Mari said proudly. "She does it all the time."

The ticket collector returned after collecting the fares. "Why don't you go up to the front?" he said. "You'll have a better view. Don't fall overboard," he warned.

We made our way to the front of the platform and leaned on the barrier. On the river were boats of various shapes and sizes. Some of them were returning to port while others headed for the open sea. Anchored in the dock were large shipping vessels from different countries.

The ticket collector joined us. "Isn't that a grand sight?" he said.

"That's the River Tees below us."

Mari was looking up at the top of the bridge.

"It's really high up there. Marlene told me that a man jumped off the top and he was killed."

"W-why d-did h-he d-do th-that?" Jeannie asked, standing back from the barrier in horror.

"That Marlene can't half spin some lies," said Katie, looking daggers at Mari.

"It's true. People jump off the top all the time, don't they Mister?" Mari asked.

"Not all the time," he said.

"Why do they do it," I asked.

"Because they are very unhappy," he said quietly.

Soon we'd crossed the water and had embarked at Port Clarence. We waved goodbye to the kindly ticket collector and made our way out of the port.

Coming to a crossroads, we looked for the signs for Hartlepool but couldn't see any. We didn't know which road to take.

"Let's go straight ahead and get away from here," Katie said.

"D- do y-you th-think th-they m-missed u-us y-yet," Jeannie asked.

I suddenly realised that I had not delivered the note to Sister Carmel. It was still in my gymslip pocket. What if Sister Mary had wanted a reply? She would be asking for me and that would give us away. I decided not to say anything.

We kept going at a fast pace. Jeannie was struggling to keep up. Then Mari said, "I've got a stitch in me side."

So we stopped for a rest.

"Hope we've taken the right road," Katie said.

"Why don't we ask someone?" I suggested.

It was beginning to get dark and I was feeling the cold. I was only wearing a thin cardigan over my gymslip.

"I'm not going to ask anyone," Katie said, "but you can if you want."

Further along the road we passed a pub. There was a lot of noise coming from inside. We could hear men's voices and the clinking of glass. And there was an overwhelming smell of tobacco and beer.

"Who dares to go in and ask the way to Hartlepool?" Mari giggled.

"N-not m-me," said Jeannie.

A couple of women came by, looking at us suspiciously. One had rollers in her hair and she stopped to ask if we were looking for someone.

"No, no," we said in unison.

We had just gone past the pub when a man in greasy overalls came walking towards us.

"Go on, ask him Mari," Katie said. "I dare you."

"Yes, go on," I said. "We might be going the wrong way."

"He's horrible and scruffy. I'm not asking him," said Mari.

"I'll ask him," I said, suddenly feeling quite brave but also concerned that we might be getting lost.

"Excuse me, could you show us the way to Hartlepool?"

He looked at me, then at the others, and grinned.

"Eeh lasses, you are going in the wrong direction.

"This is the Works Road. You'll need to go back the way and get onto the Tees Road."

"Oh no," I sighed. My feet were sore.

We had no choice but to retrace our steps. We followed him back as far as the pub, then carried on to the crossroads.

The road that we eventually took was deserted except for the lorries that trundled past. We kept our heads down. God knows what those lorry drivers must have thought, seeing four girls on this desolate road.

"T-they m-might t-tell th-the p-police," Jeannie said.

As we walked along, we talked about our families. Katie's mother had remarried and had gone on to have three more children.

"Me stepfather only wants his own kids," she said. "I've two older brothers but they're with their dad."

"Couldn't you have gone and lived with him?" I asked.

"Nah, he didn't want me. He's not me dad," she explained.

"That's why I was put in Nazzie House. I don't know where me dad is.

"Only me granny cares about me. But she isn't well. Me mam says that she's soft in the head."

Mari had no contact whatsoever with any family.

"I'm nobody's child," she said sadly.

Jeannie said that she'd gone to sleep one night in her own bed at home. And when she'd woken up she was in Nazzie House.

"You still have nightmares," I said, remembering the times that she'd woken me up in the night.

"I-I w-wish I-I c-could t-talk p-properly," she said.

I told them about my mother, here one minute and gone the next.

Yes, we were a group of abandoned kids all right.

Lost in our own thoughts, we walked on for a while in silence.

Then Mari said, "I can smell the sea. We must be near Seaton Carew."

"I'm h-hungry," Jeannie grumbled.

"Bet they'll have had supper by now," Mari said.

"Don't think about food," Katie said.

"When we get to me granny's, we'll have a feast."

I took the Fruit Pastilles from my pocket and offered them round.

We walked on until we came to a dockyard where a large cargo boat was anchored. It had the name S-K-R-I-P-A across its bow.

"That's a strange name," Katie remarked.

"It's probably foreign," I said.

"Oooh, how exciting," Mari enthused. "Let's get on."

"W-we m-might f-find s-some f-food," Jeannie said.

"It might take off with us on board," I warned.

"If it starts to move, we'll scarper," Mari said.

"If it starts to move," I said, "we will have to jump overboard."

"What, into the water?" Katie asked.

"I c-cant s-swim," Jeannie said nervously.

"You can stay here and wait for us if you don't want to come on board," Mari said.

"No, it's best if we all stay together," I said. "Come on Jeannie, we'll look after you."

I'd never been on a boat that big and I was curious. I decided to "just have a look." Hesitantly, we followed Mari up the ramp.

"A-are w-we s-stowing a-away?" Jeannie asked.

We clambered up on deck. It was eerily quiet, not a soul was in sight.

"I'm definitely not going any further," Katie said.

"N-nor m-me," Jeannie shivered.

"I'm going to see what's down there," Mari said, pointing into the distance.

"Anne, are you coming with me?"

I wanted to say yes, but there was an alarm going off in my head.

"No, I think we'd better get off now," I said.

"Oh, you are all cowards. I'll go and have a look myself then."

"You can't go off on your own," I warned.

"Oh, can't I?" she said stubbornly, and she started to walk away.

"Come back Mari, come back," we all yelled at her. "It might be dangerous."

A gang of men appeared from out of the mist. Our shouting must have alerted the crew. They came running towards us, yelling in a foreign language.

"Quick, run for it," Katie shouted.

Poor Jeannie was glued to the spot, too frightened to move. One of the sailors grabbed hold of her.

Mari tried to run but she didn't get far.

You should have heard her yelling.

"Get off me. I'll tell me mam, and me dad will beat you up."

She had caught the acting bug all right.

I could have made a run for it, but I was tired, cold and hungry.

And I was also dreading the reaction of the nuns when we got back.

The crewmen surrounded us.

"What you doin'? Where you live?" a burly man asked in broken English. We didn't answer.

Another member of the crew arrived with a man in uniform, whom I presumed was the guard.

"What are you lasses doing here?" he asked in amazement.

"We've run away from Nazzie House," Mari said defiantly.

"Nazzie House, where's that?" he asked.

"It's Nazareth House," I corrected him.

"Isn't that the children's home?"

"Yes," I nodded.

"I'm going to have to call the police," he said. "You can't stay here. It's too dangerous."

He explained our dilemma to the burly man who could speak a little English. He in turn translated to the crew. They looked at us and then smiled sympathetically. One of the crew gave each of us some chocolate.

When the police arrived we were taken to the police station in two police cars. Unlike the crewmen, they were not sympathetic at all. They had been searching for us for hours.

It was around midnight when we got back to Nazareth House. Mother Superior and Sister Mary were waiting in the parlour. It was all nice and polite talk while the policemen were there. But when they had gone we were severely reprimanded. I was told to go and scrub the corridor.

It was well after midnight and I was on my hands and knees scrubbing the long corridor on my own. I was hungry, tired and I wanted my bed. I'd got half way through the cleaning when Sister Mary came down the corridor.

"Go to bed," she yawned.

"I'll deal with you in the morning, and you will have no pocket money for a week."

I went up to the dormitory and was about to get in my bed. But there was somebody sleeping in it.

"I'm so glad to see you," my sister whispered.

"I was worried about you. Why did you run away?"

"I'll tell you in the morning. Who's in my bed?"

"It's a new girl. She was brought in this evening. There was no bed for her so they put her in yours."

"Where am I going to sleep?"

"You can come in with me. We'll sort it out in the morning."

We were quite squashed in the single bed. But I was so tired that I soon fell asleep.

I had to find another bed in another dormitory.

For the next few weeks, whenever Sister Mary saw me she wouldn't let me forget it. "I expected more from you," she would say.

CHAPTER 15

The Kindness of Strangers

There were many volunteers who helped to brighten our lives. One was Miss Molly Hackett. She set up the Girl Guides group at Nazareth House and was our leader. Because of her, we had more opportunities to venture outside of the orphanage.

In Bob-a-Job week she would take us to her friends and neighbours' homes. And we would earn funds for our group by doing odd-jobs like sweeping the leaves from the path. It wasn't a strenuous task and we had fun. It was much better than the chores that we had to do in the home.

She would also take the Girl Guides carol singing in the weeks leading up to Christmas. We would arrive at her home and her mother would come out and listen to our "wonderful singing." Most of the girls were in the choir so we could at least sing in tune.

The Girl Guides put on a nativity play at Christmas and all the residents including the nuns came to see it. I enjoyed the play sessions that she organised. The games such as 'swab the deck' were very popular and we would sit in a ring around a pretend camp fire while she told us interesting stories like Hiawatha.

We would always close the session with the Guide Creed:

I Promise on my honour, to do my best, to do my duty,

to God and the Queen. To help other people at all times, and to obey the Guide law.

There was another pleasant young lady called Miss Button who came to Nazareth House to give the girls free ballet and tap dancing lessons. Those girls who showed real promise were entered into dance competitions. This was a wonderful opportunity which they would not have had otherwise, and quite a few of the girls won medals.

Elizabeth joined the tap dancing classes, which she enjoyed, and I attended the ballet classes, albeit reluctantly. Much to the amusement of Mari and Jeannie, I was dragged there by my sister who felt that I should be "doing something." I wasn't keen; ballet was for cissies, I thought. But I still remember the five basic steps to this day.

Miss Kitty Lappin was instrumental in setting up the Legion of Mary. Every Wednesday, two of the girls would take it in turns to meet her at the bus stop. I remember she had dainty feet and wore high heels that would clatter on the pavement as she walked.

We had to pay subs each week out of our pocket money, and this would be put in the collection box at the meeting. Unfortunately, there was a coin machine that sold sweets near the bus stop. Mari and I couldn't resist and would use some of our sub money to buy sweets.

When the collection money was added up at the end of the meeting it was always short. "Who has not put their subs in?" Sister Mary would shout. Bernadette Whelan, who was the treasurer, found a way of solving the problem. We had to write our initials on the theepence coin. That put an end to our sweet treat.

The Knights of Saint Columbus and local firms would organise many events for us throughout the year.

We looked forward to the Christmas Concert that these volunteers put on at the end of the year. They kept us entertained with various performances.

The popular Mr. McCormack would introduce each act and he always had something amusing to say.

One song that he sang was "Roll out the Barrel" and, encouraged by him, we would all join in.

Another favourite was "The Rose of Killarney" which must have been requested by the nuns. Sister Agnes would get misty-eyed when he sang that tune.

The group of volunteers would organise games such as musical chairs and pass-the-parcel. Then Father Christmas would arrive amid much fanfare and hand out presents and sweets to the children.

At the end of the night, a net full of balloons would be let down from the ceiling and we would scamper to grab a balloon. There would be lots of popping sounds as they burst.

We were also taken to the Smiths Dock's annual gala day and coach loads of children from the home would be bussed to the event. It was a great day out.

There, we watched children in colourful costumes marching in a band. I was fascinated watching the girls twirling a baton around, throwing it in the air and catching it. I had never seen anything like it. Our processions were never like that.

The children from Nazareth House were encouraged to take part in the many games and races. There was a roll-a-penny stall and on the coconut shy I had my first taste of a coconut, which didn't impress me at all. It was quite watery.

My favourite memory is of the day I went on the ride that we called the 'aerial flight'. It was something like what the army would use in training exercises.

You climbed up the steps, then at the top you took hold of a wooden handle bar that was attached to an overhead wire. You hung on for dear life as you slid down all the way to the bottom. When you were nearing the end you had to put your feet out in front of you, or you would have gone head first into the sacking. (No health and safety rules here.) My sister wouldn't go near it. I had a couple of goes, it was brilliant and I loved it.

On a Bank Holiday at the end of June (the day always seemed to fall on the 29th which was the Feast Day of Saints Peter and Paul), Mr. Griffiths, one of the volunteers, would organise outings to the seaside for the children.

Every year we went to a different resort. It was either Seaton Carew, Whitley Bay, Tynemouth, South Shields or Seaburn.

There would be quite a few coaches setting off from Nazareth House, carrying the old folks as well as the children.

We were never told which seaside resort we were heading for. We had to guess; even the bus driver pretended that he didn't know. (Sometimes he got lost, so maybe he wasn't pretending after all.)

On the bus on the way there, we always sang this song:
We don't know where we're going 'til we're there
There's lots and lots of rumours in the air

We heard the Captain say

We're on the road today

But we don't know where we're going 'til we're there.

At the seaside, one of the volunteers using a cine camera would take moving pictures of us while we were playing games, building sandcastles or paddling in the sea. Then at the Christmas concert at the end of year these images would be shown on the big screen and there would be shouts of "That's me!" when we recognised ourselves.

A man from the Variety Club of Great Britain would put films on for the children. Norman Wisdom had us in stitches. Shirley Temple was "dead canny" we all agreed when we watched her in The Good Ship Lollipop.

Other black and white films such as Carry on Teacher were also shown, as were plenty of war films which we found boring.

Each year, an enormous chocolate Easter egg would be donated to the home. But we only received a small piece as it had to be shared among too many children. We made do with a paste egg which we would decorate and roll down the embankment.

We did not get new clothes in Nazareth House. They were usually hand-me-downs. As one girl grew out of her dress or uniform it would be given to another girl.

Therefore, one year when brand new jumpers and plastic sandals were donated for every girl, we were elated.

There were also families who would take children out to their own homes for Sunday tea.

I was lucky enough to be chosen along with another girl to have tea with a Mr. and Mrs. Atkinson. They had a 'posh' house in Acklam and we were made to feel very welcome.

We had ham sandwiches, cakes and ice cream – a rare treat indeed. Of course, they were curious about our lives in Nazareth House and asked lots of questions. But we were always careful not to say too much as it would have got us into trouble with the nuns.

CHAPTER 16

Sweet William

I got to know William, my first boyfriend, through Mari because she fancied his friend Paul. I was about thirteen years of age. The lads often came to our school on their bicycles as they lived some distance away. It started off innocently enough, with Mari whistling at them as they cycled past. They would ignore her. But she would continue to shout:

"Give us a go of your bell."

Then one morning, they came along pushing their bicycles as William had a punctured tyre. That was the start of our 'romance'.

At first I would just stand with Mari as she flirted with Paul and I ignored William. I was too shy to start a conversation and lads were alien to me.

Eventually we got to talk to each other, although we didn't get off to a good start as the first thing he asked was why I was in Nazareth House. I blushed down to the roots and told him to mind his own business, and I ignored him after that. When Mari would stop to talk to Paul, I just walked on.

One day he followed me. "I didn't mean to be nosy," he said shyly.

After that, when he came by on his bicycle he would slow down so we could have a chat. The lads would ask us about our life in Nazareth House. They were amazed when we told them about all the chores we had to do before and after school.

"I just have to roll out of bed and me mam gives us breakfast," William said.

"I don't have to do nowt," Paul said. Our lifestyles were worlds apart.

We didn't have the freedom that the 'outside girls' had, so there would be no question of us meeting out of school hours. However, we did manage to spend a short time together in Albert Park one Saturday. We were allowed out to the sweet shop to spend our pocket money so Mari and I sneaked to the park to spend time with our 'boyfriends'. It was innocent enough and there were no holding hands. We just walked around the park and they followed behind. We were careful not to be seen with them.

The 'courtship' didn't last long.

Pam Cahill, who was older than Mari and me, would sneak out sometimes to meet her boyfriend Tom, who happened to be Paul's cousin. They would meet in the 'cabbage garden'. This was a large, walled garden at the back of Nazareth House. Vegetables and rhubarb used to be grown there during the war, but now it was overgrown and derelict.

Tom would climb over the wall, and he and Pam would spend time canoodling. She was in charge of locking the back door at night and handing the keys back to one of the nuns.

One evening I was in the playground with Mari. We were allowed to stay out a little later now we were older, but when the bell rang we had to go in. We were sat on a roundabout called the Ocean Wave. Pam came rushing over all excited. "Tom's waiting for me in the cabbage garden."

"Guess who's with him," she said mischievously.

"Mother Superior?" I laughed, wondering how she'd managed to sneak out to meet Tom without getting caught when there were so many spies about.

"It's Paul and William. They've asked me to come and get you."

Mari was all for it. "Ooh, let's go."

I was more reticent. The cabbage garden was out of bounds, it would be risky. What would we say if we were caught? Some girls were playing netball and were preoccupied with the game but there were other girls just standing about. They could 'rat' on us.

A girl called Doreen came up to us. She sensed that we were up to something.

"What's up," she asked.

"Nothing," Pam said.

"I know that lad's in the cabbage garden, isn't he?"

"How do you know?" Pam asked.

"I'm not daft. Don't worry, I won't say anything."

Doreen was one of the senior girls. She would be leaving school at the end of term and was going to live with relatives in Saltburn.

She had ginger hair and freckles and a plump, round face and ruddy complexion which gave her a healthy glow. She was kind-hearted.

If one of the younger girls was being chastised she wouldn't hesitate to confront the bully. She wouldn't start a fight but would not back down if challenged. Most of the time she was placid, but if she lost her temper sparks would fly.

"Why don't you go and meet him?" Doreen asked.

"I'm waiting for these two," Pam remarked.

"There's two other lads turned up and they want to see Anne and Mari." Doreen looked at me in surprise.

"What! You've got a boyfriend, Anne Traynor?"

I blushed and didn't answer.

"Eh, you kept that quiet."

Yes, I thought. I wasn't exactly going to go telling everyone and have it get back to the nuns.

"And you as well," she said to Mari. "A right pair you are," she laughed.

"Only a few weeks to go and I'll be out of this prison," she said, wistfully.

"You'll be able to go out on dates with boys," Mari said enviously.

"Nah, I'm not interested, they're too much trouble."

"How do you know?" Pam asked.

"I just do."

"Don't be getting these lasses into any bother," she said to Pam.

"We're not going to do anything." I was annoyed at her implication.

"Are you going to go and meet these lads then? You'd better get a move on before the bell goes."

"How are we going to get in there without being seen?" Mari asked.

"I'll throw the ball over the wall," Doreen said,

"accidentally, of course, and you three can go and look for it. I'll keep a lookout till the bell goes."

"Ah thanks Doreen, you're a pal," Pam grinned.

William gave me a cheeky grin when he saw me.

"I can't stay long. If the nuns find us missing we've had it," I said.

"Yeah, if we're caught we'll be scrubbing the scullery floor for a week," laughed Mari, grabbing hold of Paul's hand.

"A whole year," Pam chipped in as she and Tom moved away.

I looked back at Nazareth House. Upstairs in the dormitories the lights were on and the younger girls were getting ready for bed.

William and I looked at each other not quite believing that this was happening. We had not spent any time on our own. I'd always had a chaperone, either Mari or Pam. I felt awkward and lost for words. He moved closer and tried to take my hand but I recoiled more in shock than anything. There was an awkward silence. I looked around and so did he.

"Wow! Look at those shooting stars," he said, suddenly pointing to the sky. Mari and Paul came running over.

"Where?" they shouted.

"Look, in that direction," William said.

We four stood gazing at this wondrous sight. It was a perfect evening for romance.

The bell rang and it was time for us to go in. I wanted to relish these few moments with William so I stayed. I'm not a kid any more, I reasoned. I was thirteen-years-old, a teenager.

After a while, I realised how dark it was getting as the

lights in the dormitory were being turned off. I started to feel panicky.

"We'd better go in," I said.

"We'll have to go now Pam," I shouted.

There was no reply.

"Come on you two love birds," Mari called, impatiently.

"The nuns will be looking for us."

A bright light was switched on and Tom came out from behind a bush. He was carrying a torch. Pam followed.

He was switching the torch on and off. Then they started fooling around and playing tigs.

"Pam, we haven't got time for messing around," I said.

But she didn't want the fun to end.

"Let's all have one game of tigs before we go," she said.

I was getting increasingly nervous as I saw more lights go off in the dormitories.

Pam and Tom carried on chasing each other; she was swinging the keys in her hand. He managed to grab them from her.

"Give us them," Pam shouted.

Tom dangled the keys above her head.

"Shall I throw them over the wall?" he teased.

"Don't you dare! Give her the keys," I demanded.

"She'll get into trouble if they're lost."

"Okay," Tom said, losing interest in the game. He threw the keys over her head.

"Go and find them then," he said petulantly.

At that moment all the lights in the dormitories went out and we were left in near darkness.

"What did you go and do that for?" I asked. "We've had

116

it now."

Tom switched the torch on and pointed it in the direction in which he had thrown the keys.

"Can you see them?" he asked.

The area was overgrown with weeds and nettles. It would be like looking for a needle in a haystack.

"We'd better find them," Pam said.

"They'll have another set, won't they?" Tom asked.

"If we are locked out, how are we going to get back in? Crickey! What if somebody has locked the back door?" I asked.

The seriousness of the situation suddenly dawned.

Pam took the torch from Tom.

"You'd better start looking, you idiot," she said.

There was no playfulness between them now.

She aimed the torch at Paul and William, who were hunched down and feeling around on the ground.

"Ouch, there's loads of nettles," groaned Paul.

"Aim the torch over here," said Mari, who thought that she had seen something shiny. There were plenty of false sightings but there was no sign of the keys. We were on our knees scanning the area with our hands. The keys couldn't be found. We were in big trouble.

"What are you going to do?" William asked. He showed more concern than the other lads.

"Don't know," I said.

Paul was helping us search at first, then he got fed up. "You're never going to find them in this light," he said.

Tom thought it was hilarious. "Boo!" he said, coming up behind Mari.

"Act your age," she snapped angrily.

William came over to me. "Will you get a bashing?" he asked.

"Bashing? Is that what you 'outsiders' call a good hiding?" I said, trying to make light of the situation. He didn't answer.

"You should make up something to tell the nuns if you're caught," Tom suggested.

"I've had it. I've lost a whole bunch of keys," Pam groaned.

"They won't be able to lock the back door or get into the store cupboard. All the cleaning stuff is kept there."

"Oh well, you won't have to do any scrubbing," Tom laughed.

"Shut up, you twit. It's your fault for throwing the keys away."

"I'm only kidding," he said defensively. "Can't you take a joke?"

He was the oldest among us, yet the most immature.

We didn't know the time and it seemed like we'd been in the cabbage garden for ages.

"What are we going to say?" I asked.

"I'll say that I lost the keys in the playground, and Mari and you were helping me look for them," Pam said.

It was a reasonable excuse. But would the nuns believe that we had been searching in the dark? The reality was that we should have been in our beds instead of canoodling with the lads in the cabbage garden. Three brazen hussies indeed!

"We had better go now," I said.

"Hope you don't get into trouble," William said.

"Aren't you going to give her a kiss before you go?" Mari said.

He hesitated, then egged on by the others he gave me a peck on the cheek.

Sweet William! Our courtship ended with our one and only kiss. "Where's my kiss?" Tom said, as he grabbed Pam.

"Get lost. I'm not talking to you."

She pushed him away.

The lads made their way to the wall.

"See you then," William said, as he climbed over the wall.

There was a thud as the three of them landed on the other side.

Unknown to we three girls, someone had noticed the boys climbing over the wall and, recognising Paul, they had given his name to the headmaster at Saint Richards. Consequently, the three of them were severely reprimanded by him and were given the cane. They were warned to stay away from us by the headmaster and their parents.

We rushed out of the cabbage garden. I was the first to reach the back door. Quietly, I turned the handle. But the door wouldn't open. It was locked. It couldn't get much worse.

"Now what do we do?" I whispered. We stood there trying to figure out what to do.

"I know," said Pam.

"Let's see if Alice is up."

Alice was the housekeeper, a spinster in her sixties. She had been brought up in the home and had spent all her working life there. Her room was just across from the parlour and it had a back door leading into the inner yard. Her duty now was to look after the parlour and to open the door to visitors when she heard the door bell ringing. She must have opened the door to countless visitors over the years, and she even remembered the day I and my sister had arrived all those years ago.

In spite of her hands that were deformed because of rheumatism, she kept the parlour spotless and well polished.

Alice knew everybody's business and loved to gossip. She was slim with grey hair and a long nose on which she would perch her spectacles when she was reading. Always neat and tidy, she wore twin suits with a necklace of tiny pearls. She often complained about her false teeth, which irritated her gums. And because she had bunions on both feet, she would ask us girls to wear her new shoes and 'break them in' for her.

The girls would run errands for her so she knew most of them. Everything was in its place in her room and she knew precisely where everything was. She slept upstairs in the staff bedroom but would often stay in the parlour until late.

We crept alongside the wall and made our way to her door.

The light was on and as we got near we could see that she was in the kitchen. Alice never drew the curtains at night, even when it was dark. It was assumed that it was because she was lonely and was always ready for a natter if anyone passed her door.

"Remember we were looking for the back door keys.

Don't slip up and mention the lads," Pam whispered.

Mari and I moved to the side and out of sight. She knocked gently on the window. Alice was startled. She looked up and saw Pam. We heard her say, "What on earth…" – the rest of the sentence was lost at the turning of the key in the lock. She opened the door slightly.

"Pam Cahill, what are you doing out at this time of night?"

She opened the door wider and Mari and I came into view. Her mouth opened wide in astonishment. But before she had time to say anything, Pam said, "Shh, Alice, please don't tell on us. I lost the keys to the back door and we've been out looking for them."

"Come in and wipe your feet. You look a mess."

Pam went in first. Mari and I followed.

"Where have you been?" she asked, looking us up and down.

"You stink to high heaven."

I caught sight of myself in the long mirror that was hanging on the wall. My clothes were smeared with muck. And there were muddy marks where I'd wiped the sweat from my face and I could feel the dirt in my fingernails.

"Did you find the keys?"

"No, no," we answered.

"And somebody's locked the door," Pam said.

"How could they have locked the door if you had the keys?" Alice asked.

"They must have had a spare key," Pam said anxiously, wanting to get away. Alice was asking too many questions.

"Has anyone been looking for us?" I asked.

"No, not that I know of. Should there have been?" she asked, looking at me inquisitively. "Did you not have permission to look for them?"

Alice was getting more suspicious by the minute.

She had seen many a girl scrubbing the scullery floor late at night, even as late as eleven o'clock, but they were never allowed outside.

"No, I didn't have permission," Pam said. "But I was scared of getting into trouble so I asked these two if they would help me find them."

"Some friend you are," she said to Pam. "If the nuns see you like this, they'd have a fit."

"We had better go upstairs now," I said, anxious to get away.

Alice was concerned. "You'd better be careful. We have visitors in the parlour. Some late arrivals were admitted tonight, the welfare brought them. Three little girls and they screamed the place down. Sister Joseph had them taken to the upstairs nursery."

"Where is she now?" I asked.

"She's in the parlour with the welfare officers."

My feet were aching. I just wanted to go to bed.

"Come on, let's go. We'll sneak up the winding staircase," I said.

We were about to leave when we heard loud voices coming from the parlour. The door opened and footsteps were heading our way.

There was no time to hide before Sister Joseph came into the room. She was surprised to see us.

"Alice, what on earth is going on?"

"They have been searching for some keys, Sister," Alice stuttered, equally taken by surprise.

"What keys?"

There was a murmur of voices in the background. Sister Joseph remembered that she had visitors.

"Would you make a pot of tea please, Alice? I want an explanation," she said. "I will deal with you three when I have finished with the visitors," and she left the room.

"There's no way I'm going to hang round and wait for her," Pam said.

"Me neither," said Mari

"Nor me," I said.

"Sister Joseph says you have to wait. What shall I tell her?" asked Alice.

"Tell her we needed the toilet," Mari said, as we quickly followed Pam out the door.

I was expecting a nun to come out of any of the rooms along the passages and catch us red-handed. Our shoes were leaving muddy footprints so we took them off and carried them.

Footsteps could be heard. We froze even though there was no place to hide.

I listened intently, wondering if the footsteps were heading towards us.

Then all went quiet.

"It must have been a ghost," Mari whispered. She grabbed hold of Pam's arm.

"Ooh save me."

"Get off me, you soft thing," Pam said.

In spite of the situation we were in and probably because

I was nervous, I got a fit of the giggles. It was contagious. Soon the three of us were in stitches.

"Eeh, stop it," Mari said. "I'm wetting myself."

"It's not funny," Pam said, her hand over her mouth trying to stifle a laugh. "I'm in big trouble losing those keys."

"We'll have to say a prayer to the patron saint of lost things. I think its Saint Jude," Mari said.

"No, he's for lost causes," I said.

"That's us," said Pam, and there was more giggling as we cautiously made our way down the passage to the winding staircase.

The winding staircase led from the ground floor up to the bedrooms. It was used mostly by the girls as the nuns tended to use the main staircase. There was just enough room for two people on each step. And there were iron railings on one side to hold on to. You could not see who was coming up the stairs or who was following behind until they were nearly on top of you. But you could hear their footsteps which made it quite spooky, especially at night.

I led the way up the staircase, followed by Pam and Mari who were linking arms.

"No more giggling," I said. "It's serious now."

There were only a few dim lights sporadically placed along the wall. On reaching the top landing we headed straight for the bathroom. I took off my clothes and wiped the dirt from myself as best as I could, and then wrapped a towel around me.

"Nite nite," I said quietly to Mari and Pam as we made our way to our dormitories. So far so good, I thought and there were no nuns about.

A girl called June Hughes was coming towards me.

She was one of the younger girls and would often walk in her sleep.

"Is that you, Anne? Where have you been?" she asked.

"No, Anne's in bed fast asleep," I whispered cheekily. "You're only dreaming."

I crept into the dormitory and made my way over to my bed. The light in Sister Wulstan's cell was on and fortunately the door to her cell was closed.

"Where have you been?" Elizabeth whispered.

"I'll tell you in the morning."

"I drew the curtains so Sister Wulstan would think you were in bed."

"Ah thanks." I put on my nightdress and got into bed.

I was so tired that I went to sleep as soon as my head hit the pillow. But I had an awful nightmare. I dreamed that I was being chased across a field by three ghosts.

When I woke up I thought that I'd wet the bed. But I had started my periods.

Now I would have to see Sister Mary and read the book about the Virgin Mary.

God bless us and save us.

CHAPTER 17

Holidays at Redcar

During the summer holidays the children from Nazareth House would stay in the coastal resort of Redcar. We stayed at the Sacred Heart School and slept on mattresses on the classroom floor. It was unusual accommodation but we loved it.

On the day of departure the senior girls would be roped in to help the removal men stack all our our mattresses, sheets and blankets into the back of a van.

This was always a fun time. The nuns would be at vespers and would leave us to it. Of course, Mari would be flirting with the young men.

"Have you got a girlfriend?" she would ask.

The removal van would go on ahead to Redcar and after lunch the children would follow on the coaches.

When we arrived at the school the classrooms had already been cleared of desks, chairs and blackboards.

The mattresses would be laid side by side in three rows. There was barely any room between them and we would have to step over other mattresses to get to our own. Not such a good thing if you were wearing sandals and traipsing sand all over the place.

The school was not far from the beach and the smell of the sea and the fresh air was invigorating. I vividly remember the excitement of it all. We still had light chores to do, but you didn't mind them so much when you remembered the fun that you were going to have afterwards.

In the mornings we would go to the local swimming baths, and in the afternoons we went to the roller-skating rink or the amusements. On the beach there was always plenty to do. There were talent shows, sandcastle competitions, donkey rides and a Punch and Judy show.

The junior girls were put under the charge of a senior girl. They had to be back at the school for six o'clock. Then they were allowed to play rounders or tigs in the schoolyard until it was time for bed. The routine was much more relaxed

There was a boating lake near the school and we would stand and watch the canoeists paddling in the water.

Some charitable organisations and businesses in Redcar were very generous. They arranged for each child to have a free ice cream and a bag of chips every day, and there were also free rides on the amusements and rowing boats. We just had to show our 'free' admission tickets that we were given. It was bliss. The kindness of strangers!

On Sundays we went to Mass at the Sacred Heart Church. I thought that it had a more 'cosy' atmosphere, and there were plump cushions to kneel on, unlike the hard, wooden kneelers at Nazareth House.

I had to write postcards to our benefactors and to Mother Superior back at Nazareth House. I was always careful not to make any spelling mistakes, as Sister Mary would get cross with me if I did.

We had our meals in the canteen which was in a prefab

across the yard from the school. We sat on benches around the wooden tables.

I envied the pupils. They were fortunate in having a school in such a nice location.

The school even had showers. (In Nazareth House they only had old-fashioned sinks and baths.) But at first we couldn't figure out how to use them. I was afraid that we would flood the place out.

We always had a cold shower as there was no hot water, but we didn't mind. We would 'dare' each other to stay under the shower for the longest time. It was ideal though if you just wanted to rinse the sand off your feet.

The junior girls were not allowed to use the showers. Maybe the nuns thought that they would drown in them.

One day a group of us decided to walk to the South Gare Lighthouse. We could see it in the distance and it didn't seem that far away, so we felt that it wasn't necessary to ask the nuns for permission. It was early in the evening when we set off across the sand. It had been a hot day and it was still warm, and now the beach was bathed in the orange glow of an evening sunset. Mari and I were in our bare feet. We'd left our shoes on the sea wall. The sand felt soft and squashy underfoot as we tramped along.

There were about eleven of us at first but as girls got tired or couldn't be bothered they simply dropped out and made their way back to the school. I wasn't one to give in that easy, and neither was Mari.

Jeannie reluctantly had decided to come along with us. As we sauntered along, we talked about what we had done that day; what amusements we had been on, and if we had any free tickets left for ice cream.

"I've been on the big dipper," Mari said proudly.

"Angela Thomas came with me and you should have heard her screaming. My ears were ringing when I got off. I thought I'd gone deaf."

We listened as she related her experience on the ride.

"It climbs up to the top and then it stops right on the edge, and you think your gonna topple over. I was in the front and I hardly dared look. But then it speeds down the track really fast and you're rattling around in your seat. I tell you, if we weren't strapped in we'd have gone flying."

"O-o-h I w-w-wouldn't g-go n-n-near i-it," Jeannie shuddered.

"I was gonna have a go but I went on the dodgem cars instead," Shirley Egan said. "There's a dishy fellow in charge, and every time he sees Penny and me he comes over and rides on the back of our car, doesn't he Pen?" she said to her friend.

"I think he fancies you, Shirl," Penny said.

"No he doesn't, it's you he fancies."

"Maybe he fancies both of you," Mari said.

"Don't you say anything to the nuns," she warned, "or any of you lot," she said looking around at us. We assured her we wouldn't. We didn't want a clip round the ear hole.

"I've been on the waltzes five times," I said.

It was my favourite amusement ride.

The girls were amazed.

"I can't go on the waltzers. It makes me dizzy," Brenda, one of the senior girls, said.

"Did you really go on the waltzes five times?"

"Yes," I nodded.

"Good grief," she said, looking at me admiringly. "I only went on it the once and I was as sick as a dog."

I was fortunate that the spinning around didn't affect me as it did some of the girls. Some had felt nauseous afterwards and had vowed never to go on the ride again.

Jeannie had gone on the ghost train with Mari, but hadn't seen anything as she had kept her head down the whole time and screamed when anything had even slightly touched her.

"I-I, w-w-was t-terrified," she said. "I-I w-wouldn't l-look I-d h-have f-fainted if I'd s-seen a g-ghost. I-It p-pulled my h-hair an' all," she said.

"That was me who did that," Mari giggled.

"Ah, that was cruel," we all said in chorus. "Poor Jeannie."

"I-t w-was y-ou?" Jeannie asked, and she stormed off in a huff heading back to the school. We shouted for her to come back but she wouldn't.

"Ah, she's taken the sulks," Mari said. "She'll come round."

We carried on walking for quite some time. I was wondering when we would reach the lighthouse, it seemed so near yet so far. A vast open space of sandy beach stretched out in front of me and my anxiety grew.

Throughout the years of living in the orphanage, I'd have episodes when an overpowering fear would come over me. My heart would start racing and I'd feel extremely anxious.

When I reached my teens I became aware that I was developing a fear of vast open spaces. It happened on the playing fields at school but I had kept it to myself. I could not have told anybody. They would have thought that I was mad. Today, I understand that this irrational fear was a phobia and the medical term for it is agoraphobia.

As we ventured further away from the relative safety of the school I could feel my panic rising. I started talking ten to the dozen about anything I could think of. I suppose it was my way of coping. If I kept myself occupied it gave me less time to think. To distract myself, I picked up a shell in the sand and put it to my ear.

"I can hear the sea," I said.

Soon the other girls copied and there was a competition to see who could find the biggest shell.

"I can't hear a thing," Mari said. "I'm still deaf, I think."

Shirley put the shell to her ear. "I can't hear the sea but I can hear old Woolly Bags calling us.

"'Where have all those girls gone? I'll have them scrubbing the scullery floor for a week. The brazen hussies'".

She mimicked Sister Wulstan so well that we all laughed.

Brenda spotted a boat out at sea and started singing "Michael Row the Boat Ashore," and we all joined in.

We carried on walking as the sky turned metal grey, and rumbling of distant thunder could be heard. Soon big drops of rain started to fall. And before long we were caught in a torrential downpour.

"Ah no, we are going to get soaked," I said.

We were out in the open with no shelter in sight. We started to run in the direction of the lighthouse, but it was getting difficult to see in the blinding rain.

"We'll have to turn back," Penny said breathlessly

"Ooh, if the tide comes in we'd have to swim back to the school," Mari said cheerfully.

"Swim?" Brenda said. "I can't even do a doggie paddle."

"It's much easier if you just float on your back," another girl chipped in.

"Gerraway, I'll get carried out to sea. Anyway, what are we talking like that for, scaring the life out of the younger lasses?"

And you as well Brenda, I thought.

"I don't want to go any further," Brenda said. "I'm turning back."

I was very relieved to hear it. "Me too!" I said, enthusiastically.

Most of the girls agreed that it was madness to go on, and being absolutely drenched the fun had gone out of our adventure. Only three of the senior girls decided to carry on. The rest of us turned and ran in the direction of the school. We reached the sea wall where Mari and I had left our sandals, but they were soaked through and we had to cross over the road in our bare feet.

On reaching the school we were very relieved to hear that the nuns had gone to church for evening mass.

CHAPTER 18

Pam Cahill is Kaylied

I was almost fifteen-years-old and had just left school. And I was working in the upstairs nursery. I'd been left in charge with Mari and Jeannie while the younger children and the nuns were out on a day trip.

We had been given a list of chores that had to be done before they returned. It was the usual tedious work.

Pam Cahill worked with us in the nursery. But it was her afternoon off.

I was mopping the floor of the long passage on my own when I heard, "Psst!"

I looked up but didn't see anyone.

"Psst!" There it was again.

I heard giggling. I looked behind me and saw someone peeping round the corner.

It was Susie Smith.

"Are there any nuns about?" she enquired.

"No," I replied.

She beckoned me over. I was curious and dropped the mop in the bucket.

"What's up, Sue?"

I was surprised to see her as she worked in the kitchen.

"It's Pam Cahill," she said.

"She's kaylied."

"She's what?"

"She's drunk, come and see."

I followed her round the corner.

Pam was leaning against the wall. She looked up through bleary eyes and when she saw me she shouted, "Hiya Anne, are there any penguins about?"

"Shush," Susie said.

"What happened to you?" I asked.

She grinned. "I'm s-sloshed."

"Oh my God, we'll have to hide you from the nuns," I said.

I was astonished. I'd never seen any of the Nazareth House girls drunk before.

"That friend of hers brought her into the kitchen," Susie explained. "Just left her with me, she did."

We looked at Pam, who was now staring at the ground and swaying back and forth.

"Look at her, she's legless," Susie said, shaking her head. "I've had to sneak her up here. It was a nightmare getting her up the winding staircase."

"Ee, I bet it was," I laughed.

"How did you get into that state, Pam?" I asked.

She gawped at me for a few moments with a blank expression on her face, then she realised that I was talking to her.

"I've had a couple of mild beers," she grinned.

"Just a couple," Susie said, "that's a laugh. I bet you've drank the pub dry."

Pam giggled. "Well, I might have had more than a couple," she said sheepishly.

"Lucky for her there's no nuns about at this moment," I said.

"They've gone on a trip with the nursery kids. There's just Mari, Jeannie and me here."

"She will have to sober up before they get back or she's had it," Susie said.

"How are we going to do that?" I asked.

"Me mam usually has a sleep," Susie said.

"Right then, Pam. You are going to have to have a lie down," I said.

"Nah, I'm alright," she giggled. "I'm alright."

"Pam, we'll have to get you out of the way before any of the nuns see you," I said sternly.

"I'm not scared of penguins!" she shouted at the top of her voice.

"Not unless they bite," she said and dissolved into fit of the giggles.

"Shush, shh," Susie and I said, although we couldn't help but laugh.

We watched as she staggered down the passageway bouncing off the walls.

"Ee, what's she like?" we both said.

She almost fell and I rushed over to help her, but she slid down to the floor.

"Help me get her up Sue, will you?" I asked.

"Can't Anne. I've got to get back to me kitchen duties or I'll be in trouble.

"I'll have to leave her with you," she said. "Get the others to help you," and she turned and ran.

Anxiously, I looked down the passageway hoping that there were no nuns about.

"Come on Pam, you don't want the nuns to see you

like this do you?"

Her eyes were glazed and out of focus and she kept swaying to and fro. I put my arms under her shoulders and tried to help her to stand up but she was too heavy.

I tried a few times to get her to her feet but to no avail. She thought it was hilarious and dissolved into fits of giggling at my attempts.

In the end I gave up.

"Don't move," I said. "I'll have to get Mari and Jeannie."

I ran down the passage and flung open the bathroom door.

Mari was cleaning the bath and Jeannie was busy sweeping the floor.

"Pam Cahill is drunk," I said breathlessly.

"She's what!" Mari exclaimed, dropping the cleaning cloth into the bath.

"She's absolutely sloshed. Come on, I need you both to help me."

We ran down the passage and turned the corner. Pam was sprawled on the ground with her legs wide open and her head leaning back against the wall. Her eyes were closed and she was falling asleep. It was such an undignified sight. I dreaded to think what might happen if any of the nuns came by at that moment.

I shook her awake.

"Come on Pam, let's get you up before any of the nuns see you."

She opened her eyes.

"Whoosh, me head's spinning."

"Ee, Pam you're kaylied," Mari laughed.

"Hiya Mari," she shouted. "Where's all the penguins?"

"Shh," I said. "The nuns will hear you."

"I'm drunk, Mari," she hiccuped.

"W-we c-can s-see th-that," Jeannie said.

"She will have to have a sleep and sober up," I said.

But that was a problem.

Our bedroom was on the top floor. How could we get her to her own bed without any of the nuns seeing her? We would have to take her across the yard which was overlooked on all sides. It would be impossible.

"We'll have to put you in one of the little one's beds," Mari said, who was finding the whole situation very amusing.

Just then the clock on the nursery wall chimed three times.

"Crikey, they will be back in an hour and we still have got loads to do," I said.

Mari and I helped her to her feet. She was wobbling all over the place but we held on to her tightly.

"Come on Pam, lets get you off the passage in case any of those penguins are about," Mari laughed.

It was a struggle but we managed to get her to the bathroom and sit her down on a chair.

"What does beer taste like?" Mari asked.

We were curious as we had never tasted alcohol before. But I knew about the effect too much of the stuff had on people, notably my mother.

"It tastes yucky at first," she slurred, putting out her tongue.

"Y-you're a-as d-daft a-as a-a b-brush," Jeannie said.

"Where did you go?" Mari asked.

Pam leaned back in the chair.

"Janice took me to the Black Lion in Stockton."

"Y-you've b-been i-in a-a p-pub?" Jeannie asked in amazement.

"There were loads of men and one of them asked me for a date," she smiled. "He was gorgeous!"

"Ooh, are you going to go out with him?" Mari asked. "What did he look like?"

Pam was grinning from ear to ear.

"He looked just like Slin Whitman," she said.

"Slin Whitman? Who the heck is he?" Mari laughed. We'd never heard of him.

"Janice has got all his records, she plays them all the time," retorted Pam.

"G-gerraway, I b-bet he's d-dead o-ld," Jeannie said.

Pam started to sing.

"When I'm calling yooo-hooo."

"Shush, shush, shush," we said.

"W-what d-do w-e do w-with her n-now?" Jeannie asked anxiously.

"Give her a drink of water," I said. "We will have to finish cleaning.

"We'll just have to keep an eye on her for now and hopefully she'll sober up soon."

Jean looked doubtful as that wouldn't be any time soon. I had to agree with her. Pam had certainly had a skinful.

"I'll have to get back to mopping the floor or it'll never be dry in time."

I hurried out of the bathroom and picked up the mop

and continued mopping the long passage.

I hadn't got very far when I heard footsteps coming along the adjacent passageway. I rushed up and peeked round the corner. It was Sister Wulstan and she was heading our way. Why is Sister Wulstan coming to the nursery? I wondered. This wasn't her domain. She usually supervised the junior and senior girls. I went tearing back down the passage to the bathroom.

"Sister Wulstan's coming."

"W-what a-are w-we g-going t-to d-do?" Jeannie stammered.

"Pam, we're going to have to hide you," I said

"Where?" Mari asked.

The toilets were next to the bathroom.

"Hide her in the there," I said. "But stay with her Mari and for god's sake keep her quiet."

"I'll try."

Mari just got her into the toilets in the nick of time. I rushed back to where I'd left the mop, but before I could reach it Sister Wulstan came around the corner.

"What's the mop doing in the middle of the floor?" she shouted.

"Erm, I had to change the water," I lied. (That's a venial sin.)

"You had better finish right now. Mother Superior will be coming here soon with important visitors."

Oh no! I said to myself. That's all we need.

She went hurrying down the passage, with her rosary beads rattling as she moved.

Jeannie was vigorously scrubbing the floor when Sister

Wulstan came into the bathroom.

"You will need to finish right now and put all the cleaning things away," she said breathlessly. "Mother Superior is coming round with important visitors.

"Where is Mari Carr?"

Jeannie dropped the brush.

"S- s-he's j-just g-gone..." Sister Wulstan didn't wait for her to finish speaking.

She went scurrying off down the passageway towards the main staircase, no doubt to warn all and sundry that Mother Superior and the visitors were on their way.

I emptied the mop bucket and put it away in the cleaning cupboard. Jeannie followed me into the toilets. Tentatively, I opened the door. Mari had her hand over Pam's mouth. She breathed a sigh of relief when she saw us.

"What a job I had keeping her trap shut. She wanted to come out and tell old Woolly Bags just what she thought of her."

"By, you are brave," I said.

"Mother Superior is coming," I said. "She has visitors with her."

"Oh no! Why didn't Susie leave her downstairs? Why did she have to bring her up here?" Mari said. Now she was panicking.

We looked at Pam, with each of us trying to fathom out how we could keep her out of the way until Mother Superior and the visitors had gone.

Pam was sat on the toilet seat, a dozy grin on her face and looking as if she hadn't a care in the world. We three were rattling our brains about what to do with her.

"You could take her down the winding staircase and keep her there until they've gone," I suggested.

"Good idea," Mari said

"I'll go and see if there are any nuns about. Or penguins..." she said grinning at Pam. She ran down the passageway but didn't get far and came running back.

"It's too late. Mother Superior's coming up the main stairway. She's got loads of visitors with her and some of them look really posh.

"Woolly Bags is with her an' all. She must have sneaked out to warn us."

"We're going to have to hide you," I said to Pam. She put a finger to her lips and started giggling again.

I tried to get her to understand the predicament we were in.

"It's no laughing matter, I mean it Pam," I said. "You will be out of a job and have nowhere to go."

"Where are we going to put her? They will probably want to inspect all the rooms," Mari asked.

"I know. She could go in the laundry room."

This was a small room where all the clean linen was kept.

"They are not likely to look in there," I said hopefully.

But there was nowhere else to put her.

"W-what if s-she s-starts s-singing?" Jeannie was anxious.

"I can always put a tape over her mouth or knock her out," Mari said.

"Ah, you wouldn't do that to me Mari, I'm your fwiend," Pam said playfully.

"Not if you get us into trouble you won't be."

Mari and I cajoled and practically dragged her into the laundry room.

"We'll let you out as soon as the visitors have gone, I promise," I said as I shoved her inside. Mari locked the door.

We heard voices coming from up the main staircase. The three of us panicked and ran in different directions.

"Do you think one of us should stay near the laundry room in case she starts yelling?" I asked.

Too late! Sister Wulstan was coming along the passage followed by Mother Superior and the visitors.

"Good afternoon," Sister Wulstan said in the voice reserved for occasions such as this. She held an arm out towards me.

"This is Anne. She does such a marvellous job keeping everything spick and span."

I gulped. "Good afternoon," I said to the visitors.

There were three men and four women.

The home relied on benefactors for its upkeep, we were constantly told. Therefore, we had to be on our best behaviour when they were around.

When they entered the room we had to immediately stop what we were doing and stand to attention and smile. If they asked us questions we had to answer politely. The nuns always seemed to be on edge though when the visitors were about, which made us girls even more nervous.

One of the men was quite old. He had white hair and bushy eyebrows.

He winked at me and I blushed. The scowl on Sister Wulstan's face showed her disapproval. I could read her thoughts, (yes, he was the male version of a brazen hussy).

Mother Superior chaperoned the visitors into the nursery followed by Sister Wulstan. There were lots of compliments coming from the visitors about how well the nursery was run. They were shown round the dormitories where the little ones slept and all was going well.

Suddenly! Loud banging could be heard coming from the laundry room, accompanied by shouts of "Let me out! Let me out!"

Jeannie, Mari and I looked at each other in horror.

Sister Wulstan left the visitors and came scurrying down the passages. "What on earth is going on?" she asked angrily.

Pam Cahill's shouts got louder.

"Let me out of here," she shouted while kicking the door.

Sister Wulstan fumbled with the door knob.

"Who is in there?" she asked irritably. She tried to open the door but it was locked.

Mari took the key out of her pocket and rushed to open the door.

It took a few turns as she was nervous with Sister Wulstan standing right behind her. The door was flung open and there amongst the clean sheets and bedding that had been dragged from the shelves sat Pam Cahill. She had been sick.

Horrified at the sight but not sure what was going on, Sister Wulstan went over to her.

"What are you doing? The very idea of it, sitting about in here and we have important visitors."

She came near to her and then recoiled in horror.

"Have you been drinking alcohol?"

"Just had a little drink," Pam giggled. She tried to get up but fell down again.

Sister Wulstan's face was a picture.

"You trollop! Just you wait until Mother Superior hears about this. Mark my words; the very idea of it," she ranted on. "You brazen hussy."

"Oh, don't be a tell-tale Sister Woolly Bags," Pam slurred.

Mari gasped, and opened her mouth to say something but quickly closed it again. Jeannie rolled her eyes.

The scene was so absurd that I got a fit of the giggles.

Not long after this episode, Pam left the home for good. I was transferred to the downstairs nursery.

CHAPTER 19

The Downstairs Nursery

The downstairs nursery took in newborn babies who were up for adoption. If they were not up for adoption they would remain in the nursery until they were about two years of age. They would then be transferred to the upstairs nursery until they were of school age, and then they would join the juniors and seniors in the main building.

I was fifteen when I started work in the lower nursery. The girls already working there were of similar age to me. There were about ten of us and the majority of the girls were outsiders. They had not been brought up in Nazareth House but had applied for the job of nursery nurse. I was excited when I was told that I would be working there. It seemed like a proper job – so different from working in the upstairs nursery.

We were given a uniform to wear which had to be kept spotlessly clean. It consisted of a blue dress, white apron and a white cap. We looked like real nurses in our smart uniform, although none of us girls had any nursing qualifications. It was hands-on experience for us.

We were taught by Sister Marisa, the main supervisor, on how to feed, wash and change the babies. Sister Aidan was her assistant, a rather tetchy Scottish nun.

Those girls like me who lived-in slept in the staff bedroom which was in the attic on the top floor. We had our own cubicles which gave some privacy, although they were not very big and gave you little space to move about. There was just enough room for a bed and a locker. The cubicles did not reach the ceiling so you could hear all that was going on in the other cubicles.

I got on well with one of the girls who was called Fay. She lived- in through the week but went home at weekends. Her father was in the army and the family were stationed at Catterick Camp, which meant that it was too far for her to travel home each night.

I envied her. She seemed so glamorous with her dyed blonde hair which sometimes showed her dark roots, and she also wore make-up. This never bothered the nuns.

If any of us Nazareth House girls had dyed our hair or wore make-up we would have been 'brazen hussies' or worse.

Fay would return after staying the weekend with her family and I would watch as she unpacked her case. Her uniform would be Persil white, crisply starched and freshly ironed by her mother.

I had no such luxury and had to wash my uniform by hand using carbolic soap. I would put it over the radiator to dry. Many times I wore it when it was still damp.

Fay would tell us about how she had spent the weekend either going to the pictures or to a dance. She talked about her boyfriend and why her parents did not approve of their relationship. Apparently, he was much older than her. One Saturday they had met in secret and had ended up snogging in the back row of the pictures.

The following Monday she wore a scarf around her neck

to hide the love bites. The nuns were told that she had a sore throat.

Fay would sneak her transistor radio into the home and we would listen to the latest rock and roll music. "The Young Ones" by Cliff Richard was a favourite of ours. We would pretend that we were The Shadows and do the dance steps while playing imaginary guitars. We got to see Cliff and the Shadows for free when they came to the Globe Theatre in Stockton. We were fortunate in that we were given front row seats.

"I Remember You" was also a popular song at the time. It was sung by Frank Ifield, who we saw in the pantomime Dick Whittington which was also on at the Globe Theatre.

Helen Shapiro's "Walking Back to Happiness" would get us all singing. She was about our age so we could identify with her. But we thought that she sang like a boy. She had such a unique voice though. She wore her hair in the latest hairstyle. It was backcombed and lacquered until it resembled a beehive. (It was much better than the monk's haircut though.)

My sister's idol was Billy Fury and we both loved listening to his record, "Halfway to Paradise."

Although we had left school, the nuns still kept a tight rein on our coming and going. We worked long hours in the nursery and were only allowed one half-day off per week. The wages I received was just pocket money, as deductions were made for my keep.

During this period of my life, I did not go out in the evenings. There was a staff-room where we older girls would congregate to watch television. Some of the popular programmes included Bonanza, Rawhide, and Coronation Street. The Doctor Kildare series starring the gorgeous Richard Chamberlain was a must.

Now we earned our own money, we were allowed out during the day to the local fish and chip shop where we would purchase a bag of chips. I'd put loads of salt and vinegar on. It was a luxury for me.

On our half-day off, we would go across the road to the skating rink in Albert Park or on the rowing boats if we could afford it.

There was a tree- lined walkway which led to the boating lake. When it was windy the trees would bend inwards forming an arcade over your head. There was something mystical about it and when I walked through my spirit would be uplifted. I could forget all the inhibitions of my life.

The first few months in the downstairs nursery were happy ones. We had lots of responsibilities looking after the tiny charges in our care. The newly born babies were swiftly adopted so there was no time to form attachments to them. They would be going to a loving home, we were told. Therefore I was pleased when they left the orphanage. It was better than becoming institutionalised like I had.

One role I was asked to take on was godmother. All babies had to be baptised before they left the home to be adopted. And because I was one of the Nazareth House girls I was asked to be godmother. I thought this odd as I would probably never see these babies again. I remember holding one beautiful baby girl who was soon to be adopted. She slept all the way through the baptism. I asked

Father Bickerstaffe if I could give her the name Anne. But I was told that the adopted parents would probably change her name anyway.

I was also godmother to Joseph, a gorgeous little boy of mixed race. He had dark curly hair, brown eyes and a lovely smile. He was not up for adoption. I would buy him clothes and toys with the little money that I earned. Sister Marisa would often tell me not to bother and not get too attached to him.

I would creep into the nursery before I went off duty and watch him sleeping. If he was awake he would give me one of those gorgeous smiles, although when I left him he would start crying and wake the other babies. This would have got me into bother with the other staff. I suppose I felt somehow responsible for my little godchild

Although it was a good thing that babies were going to good homes, I often wondered about their natural parents, especially the mothers. There was a general consensus that the mothers were usually young, unmarried and had been abandoned by the father of the child. There were rumours that one young mother had screamed the place down when they had taken the baby from her and they had to sedate her. I felt empathy with this young girl, although our roles were reversed. It was me who was crying for my mother all those years ago.

One little boy that I was fond of was a blond, blue-eyed boy called Jimmy. He was about eighteen-months-old. It was assumed that he had been adopted at birth, but was brought back to the orphanage after it was discovered he was blind. I would come to his cot in the morning and whisper his name so as not to startle him. He would turn his little face to the side when he heard me, and as my fingers moved along the rails. I would call his name a little louder. He would listen intently to my voice, a smile spreading across his face. And then when I slowly let down the gate and scooped him into my arms and said, "Good morning Jimmy," he would explode into laughter.

He loved playing with water. I would sit him at the sink and his little hands would be slapping the water, and when it splashed on his face it would startle him then he would giggle.

Jimmy needed one-to-one attention, but with so many other babies and children to attend to it was difficult. He would be frustrated and have fits of screaming which would upset me. I would say that if nobody wanted him then I would adopt him when I was older.

He was eventually taken to a home for children who had special needs.

CHAPTER 20

Job Interview

I enjoyed working with the babies and children. But I was a restless teenager and I was not getting on with the two nuns in charge of the nursery. I suppose that I saw them as part of the problem. They were careful not to upset the outside girls, so if anything went wrong in the nursery which involved one of the Nazareth House girls she would ultimately get the blame. It happened to me a few times and I thought this was grossly unfair. I tried to remonstrate with Sister Aidan but was told that I "should know better."

I wanted to be free of the constraints imposed on me. I decided to leave the orphanage and find other employment. One way out was to find a live-in position. Our local hospital was advertising for nursing staff and accommodation was included. I decided to go there and ask for a job.

On my half-day off I turned up at Middlesbrough General Hospital wearing my nursery uniform.

We were not allowed to wear our uniform outside of Nazareth House and if I'd been caught I would have been reprimanded and had wages deducted from my pay. Still, I was undeterred and I wore my long coat to disguise it. I had a plan.

I didn't have an appointment. I intended to go to the hospital and ask to see the matron. She needed nurses and

I would just make one request – to be allowed to work with babies and children.

Getting into the hospital was daunting. I did not want to use the main entrance in case anybody from Nazareth House saw me and then informed the nuns. I found an entrance at the back and went inside. I went up a flight of stairs which brought me to a long corridor which led to the wards. I was confronted by an irate nursing sister who told me that I had no right to be there. She didn't gave me a chance to explain what I was doing there, she just told me to go. I made my way back down the stairs feeling quite dejected. I was on the verge of giving up but then I thought that this may be my only chance.

Outside, I made my way round to the front. I took a deep breath and ran up the steps that led to the main entrance.

I told the middle-aged woman at the reception desk that I had come to see the matron about becoming a nurse. She looked at me and frowned. "Are you old enough?" she asked.

I was taken aback. Old enough? I was fifteen years of age.

I'd had a lifetime of looking after children and in the last year tiny babies as well. I probably had more experience than she had.

I opened my coat to reveal my nursery uniform.

"I'm already working as a children's nurse," I said.

She told me to go and sit in the waiting area.

There was a large clock on the wall. Fifteen minutes went by, which was long enough for the doubts to creep in. Had I made the right decision to come here?

It didn't help that the receptionist kept looking over at me when talking on the telephone. I don't think she quite knew what to make of this young girl in an unfamiliar nurses uniform. She called me over to the reception desk.

"Matron will see you. She is sending one of the nurses down to fetch you."

Eventually, a young nurse arrived. She looked at my uniform and enquired what hospital I worked for.

"I'm a nursery nurse at Nazareth House." She was puzzled.

"Isn't that the children's home?"

"Yes, I work with babies and children."

"Come with me," she said.

I followed her up a flight of stairs and along a corridor to the matron's room. She knocked on the door and a rather pleasant voice shouted, "Come in."

The door was opened and I was introduced as the girl who wanted to see Matron about a nursing post.

Matron was sitting behind a desk. Her dark wavy hair was tucked under a crisp, white cap and she was wearing a blue dress with a watch attached to the upper pocket. The nurse that had brought me here left the room, closing the door quietly behind me.

Matron smiled at me and asked me to sit down. I liked her instantly. I felt confident.

"So you wish to join our nursing staff," she said. "I have been told that you are already working as a nurse."

"Yes, I work in the nursery at Nazareth House."

"Is that the uniform?" she asked. "It's very smart."

I nodded. I was pleased that I had washed and ironed it

that morning. I had even managed to get some starch from the laundry and had dipped my white apron in it. It had made a difference.

"How long have you been working at the nursery?"

"Just over a year. I work with babies and children up to two years of age," I said proudly.

"Is it your first employment?"

"No, I worked in the upstairs nursery before that."

"The upstairs nursery?" she enquired.

"That's for the older children."

"How old?"

"They come up from the downstairs nursery when they are about two years of age, then they stay with us until they are ready to start school."

"How long did you work there?"

I hesitated. The questions were getting more probing.

"About one year," I said hesitantly.

She was looking at me not unkindly but inquisitively.

"You say that you want to work with children. Why, then, do you want to leave your present employment?"

"I want to live somewhere different," I blurted out. Oh that wasn't a good answer, I thought.

"Do you not live at home?"

"No, I live-in."

Then she asked the question that I was dreading.

"Are you a Nazareth House girl?"

"Er, yes," I said, feeling my face flush at the humiliation of having to admit it.

"How old are you?"

"I'm fifteen."

"Oh! I'm afraid that you are too young. We only take girls who are aged eighteen or above."

I was disappointed and it showed.

"I'm so sorry," she said sympathetically.

"You are welcome to enrol when you are older. I'm sure with all the experience you will have gained it would help you get on the course."

There was silence in the room as I tried to come to terms with reality. I was not expecting this; I had just assumed that with my experience I would be accepted. It had not occurred to me that I would not be old enough. What an idiot!

I made my way down the corridor and out of the hospital. This was my chance to escape and it had all come to nothing.

Later, sitting on my bed in the cubicle and reflecting on the events of the day, I didn't feel so bad. I'd had a good chance of being accepted on the nursing course. It was just my age that went against me.

The problem was I wouldn't be eighteen for another three years: that was too long to wait. I was impatient to leave. I would have to try elsewhere. Still, that interview with the matron had boosted my confidence. I grinned at the audacity of it all. Walking into Middlesborough General Hospital in my nursery uniform and asking the matron to give me a job. One brazen hussy indeed.

I had made up my mind though that I was going to leave Nazareth House. I did not want to end up like some of the women who had spent all their lives in the orphanage.

I saw a job advertisement in the Evening Gazette. A

young couple who lived on a farm were looking for a live-in nanny to look after their four children. It seemed ideal so I decided to make enquiries.

I telephoned the number given and a woman asked me to come for an interview.

A week later, accompanied by my sister, I got on the train which would take me to Middleton St. George.

When we arrived at our destination we were met by Mrs. Russell. We got in her car and she drove us to the farm. It was out in the countryside and surrounded by green fields. I wasn't so sure that I wanted to live in such an isolated spot.

She introduced me to her four children. They were all girls under the age of ten. I was shown around the living quarters.

Unfortunately, I would be sharing the same bedroom as the girls. They slept in bunk beds and there was a single bed for me.

The girls were canny and chatty.

"Are you coming to live here?" they kept asking me.

They were jumping up and down on the beds and were so rowdy. I was thinking that I wouldn't get any sleep.

Still, I felt that I had no choice but to accept the job if I wanted to leave Nazareth House. It was a start and if I was not happy I could look elsewhere.

But first I would need the permission of the nuns, as I was still under their legal guardianship.

It took me a few days before I plucked up the courage to tell Sister Marisa that I had found another job. She was very angry that I had actually gone to the farm and she was going to report me to Mother Superior. She went into the nursery and I heard her telling Sister Aidan about me.

I don't know if going for the interview at the hospital and the farm gave me the confidence. But I suddenly decided that I would go and see Mother Superior myself and hand my notice in.

CHAPTER 21

Leaving

The girls in Nazareth House did not have much contact with the Mother Superior. We would either see her in church or when she came to inspect the children or to show any visitors around.

This Mother Superior had only been with us for a short while and there were rumours that she was 'canny' so I presumed that she would be approachable.

Her room was near to the parlour which overlooked the main entrance.

Alice saw me standing outside the door.

"What are you doing there?" she asked.

"I'm going to see Mother Superior," I said. "I'm leaving."

Her mouth opened wide. She was shocked and I suspect rather envious, as she had lived in the home most of her life.

I knocked on the door.

"Just a minute," a voice said.

I was nervous but I was determined to go through with it.

The door opened and a nun came out of the room. She looked surprised to see me. It was rare to see any of the girls coming to see Mother Superior without a nun chaperoning her.

"Are you waiting to see Mother Superior?" she asked.

"Yes, Sister," I said boldly.

"You had better go in then," she said.

When I entered the room, Mother Superior was sitting behind a big old-fashioned desk. There was a large portrait of a nun hanging on the wall. This was the founder of the order of the Poor Sisters of Nazareth. I did not know anything about how the order had originated and now I was looking at its creator. There was a grim look on her face and the beady eyes seemed to look at me disapprovingly. I got the feeling that she would have been another one who would have had you scrubbing the scullery floor for the slightest wrongdoing.

Mother Superior struggled to stand up. She seemed weighed down by the nun's habit, the rosary beads and the large wooden cross that she wore around her neck. But she smiled pleasantly.

"Good afternoon, what do you want?" she asked.

I told her that I was unhappy working in the downstairs nursery and that I wanted to leave. I rambled on, telling her about the interview that I'd had with the matron and her telling me to apply for a job when I was older. I told her about my going to the farm.

"I want to work with the children there," I said.

She listened patiently and didn't interrupt. When I'd finished talking I was out of breath and my face was flushed.

"I'll see what I can do my child," that's all she said.

It was only after I had left her room that I realised that she hadn't even asked me my name.

Later that evening, Mother Superior told Sister Marisa

and Sister Aidan that a "good looking" girl had been to see her. They thought she was talking about another girl called Eileen who also worked in the nursery. But when they found out it was me they were surprised. Maybe they didn't think I was pretty. But then beauty is in the eye of the beholder.

Mother Superior had at least listened to my concerns and she'd arranged for two nuns to visit the farm and find out if it would be suitable employment for me. They reported back that:

"It would be slave labour."

Oh the irony! "And she wouldn't even have her own room."

More 'suitable' employment had to be found as I was determined to leave. It was decided that I would live and work in Saint Teresa's Home. It was situated in Marton Road in Middlesbrough and not too far from Nazareth House. This establishment was not run by the nuns. Although it came under the auspices of the Catholic diocese, it was more like a family run home. There were boys and girls of mixed ages who were in the care of a house mother.

It would be an ideal base for me to venture out into the world.

In the spring of 1964, I left Nazareth House to take up my new job at Saint Teresa's.

I stood on the steps at the main entrance remembering that time almost thirteen years ago when Raphy had brought me and my sister here.

I had said my goodbyes to the girls that had shared my

upbringing. They too would be leaving to make their own way in the outside world.

I was looking forward to a brighter future. I was nervous but I had no regrets. It was time to start a new chapter in my life.

The years ahead would see me living in a big city. I would experience life on the edge. It was the time of The Beatles, the mini-skirt and love.

I would have my first taste of alcohol. And on many occasions I too would end up 'kaylied'. There would be times when Sister Wulstan's words would echo through my addled brain: "You brazen hussy!"

New book by the Author

DON'T LET THE RIFF-RAFF IN

It is 1966 seventeen-year-old Anne Traynor has left Nazareth House the orphanage where she spent thirteen years of her life.

Now free from the constrains imposed on her by the nuns. She is able to make her own way in the world. As a bridesmaid at her sister Elizabeth's wedding she meets Katie who has split up from her long-term boyfriend.

They are both at a crossroads in their lives and looking for adventure so with the impetuous of youth they decide to leave the north-east and head for the bright lights of Manchester.

They board a train from Middlesbrough railway station with only a packet of crisps a carton of milk and very little money.

On arrival in Manchester they look for cheap accommodation to rent. The only suitable digs they can find is a bed-sit in Cheetham Hill. It is owned by Jewish landlady Mrs Lowe who runs a respectable house and no riffraff's allowed. But all is not what it seems, why do its tenants call it the Den Of iniquity?

They include Liam a young gay lad who has an off/on relationship with Robbie his violent bisexual lover. The charismatic Faye and her partner Jo and Tania who rents a bedsit overlooking the back garden so she can look out for her clients when they call.

Then there's Scots Billy and Dougie a couple of petty thieves and the police are frequent visitors to their doors.

On the top floor lives an old man a holocaust survivor. The nights are frequently broken by his loud screams as in his nightmares he relives the horrors of the concentration camps.

Anne and Katie only plan on staying until they find work and can afford a decent bed-sit. But their lives soon become intertwined with those of the other tenants.

Naive and innocent Anne is plummeted into a colourful world, which is completely at odds with her strict Catholic upbringing and will change her forever.

This is the sequel to *Memoirs of a Nazareth House Girl*.